My Louise

My Louise

A Memoir

DAVID COLLINS

To Aunt Joanne + Uncle Jim —

Fondly,

[signature]

Ontario Review Press ✦ Princeton, NJ

Oct. '02

Ontario Review Press
9 Honey Brook Drive
Princeton, NJ 08540

Distributed by W. W. Norton & Co.
500 Fifth Avenue
New York, NY 10110

Library of Congress Cataloging-in-Publication Data

Collins, David, 1962–
    My Louise : a memoir / by David Collins.—1st ed.
        p. cm.
    ISBN 0-86538-107-0
    1. Collins, Louise—Health. 2. Breast—Cancer—Patients—
Michigan—Biography. I. Title.

  RC280.B8 C5993 2002
  362.1'9699449'0092—dc21
  [B]
                                                          2002074893

First Edition

ACKNOWLEDGMENTS

This book's serendipitous route toward publication owes much to the encouragement and talents of several people, and I am deeply grateful to my sister, Susan Collins Thoms and her friend Laura Philpot Benedict—talented writers and editors both—as well as to the fine writer John U. Bacon, my agent, Carol Mann, and my editor and publisher Raymond J. Smith. I would also like to acknowledge my colleagues past and present at Gale, especially Peter Gareffa and the gang at St. James Press; and thanks as well to the friends who have helped in so many ways in the past months and years, including Lisa Deshantz-Cook, Sarah Lucas, Maggie Patton, and Kamela Torvinen; to Stacy McConnell; to Patti and Michael Chetcuti; to my good friends since our days at Michigan, John Bonnell, Anthony Domenick, and Michael Dunne; and to Marta Kwiatek; my gratitude to Louise's mother, Dorothy Walton Mooney, and to Jed, David, and Mindy Mooney; to my multitude of siblings—Cathy and her husband Winston; to Jane and Terri and Jim and his wife Theresa; to Tim, for so much help, and his wife Susan; again to Sue and her husband Bill; and finally to Mike and his wife Barb for giving us friendship and a second home; a very special thank you to my parents, James and Eileen Collins, whose example is like a mountain to us all; and lastly all my love forever and always to Robin: *you came to save me—and you have—now live your life and be happy.*

This book is for

Robin Ryther Collins

and of course

for Louise

*"A flower falls, even though we love it;
and a weed grows, even though we do not love it."*
—Dogen

My Louise

I

Ice

1

Both the beginning and the end of the first half of my life were signaled by the sound of my father's footsteps on the stairs.

That first time, I can only fathom. I came from Nowhere in the ordinary way. Like so many children born into the large, Irish-Catholic families that seemed to explode like popcorn in the middle of this last century, I was an unplanned and entirely welcome consequence of a sprawling, provident love. It was an early afternoon of 1962, about this time of year—chalk-cold in winter, the sky a forgotten gray, in the air a longing for spring. The light was bitter and failing, not even trying really. My mother (to my father, his wife) was upstairs, maybe taking a nap. The house was full of six children between the ages of nine and two. It was Saturday. My father was tired from working all week, wanted to take a nap himself—longed to ascend, if only for an hour, above all that noise which made him happy. He folded his newspaper, wandered into the kitchen, drank a glass of water as he gazed absently out over the snow-covered lawns—and headed up.

And then there it was, audible to nobody probably, except himself: the sound, slow and heavy, of my father's footsteps on the stairs. Soon after, I got started.

Thirty-five years later. Again the sound of my father's footsteps on the stairs. This time I was there to hear it. It was warm in the afternoon (again in my father's house), late autumn, the day after Thanksgiving, still light in the room where I lay, though the shades were drawn. The house was clean, bright, big: white carpeting, oak floors, tall windows all around—so comfortable, like a hotel or an inn with its soft furniture and quiet, empty spaces. I was trying to go to sleep in an upstairs room, had just lain down, eyes closed but awake, waiting for the phone to ring, for the pause, and then the sound of footsteps on the stairs.

My wife, my Louise, was dying in a hospice nearby. I had spent the previous night with her. Two of my brothers had come with me and sat with me, the three of us sleeping a little when we could in our chairs, propped up stiffly under heavy blankets, weary and confused—as respectful and mournful and awed (or so I imagined then) as the apostles who waited for Jesus in his garden.

The night passed that way, and at nine o'clock in the morning my mother came to the hospice to relieve me, to keep watch. I had returned to my parents' house, where my daughter had slept, to see her, and to get her packed up and say goodbye before she headed off to her other grand-mother's across town.

I was exhausted, petrified to stone, needed to get out of there for a while. Louise was going to die that day and I knew it. I didn't know if I could go back, didn't know if I wanted to. Something was ending. It had been long and hard. I was all jammed up, couldn't find a spot. I wanted it to end because it had to end, and yet I did not want the new thing—the time without her—to begin. Certainly the moment was unbearable as well. Time reaching off in echoes of ghostly, hollow laughter in all directions, and what I learned that day is that there surely isn't any escaping the direct blow of any singular, obvious moment. If there was I would have found it. Just out of desperation I would have found a way out.

When I left her she was still breathing—deep, gape-mouthed breaths with too much time between them, like a fish lying on the banks of a river, desperate and clinging with no other purpose than the satisfaction of an instinct older than the first river—but she was already gone. I kissed her, put my cheek up next to hers, and whispered in her ear. "I'll see you again. Someday."

It was like calling in through the window of an abandoned house. She wasn't in there anymore. She was everywhere *but* in there, in that place where I remembered her. I was going to miss that house. I had taken comfort there, had placed my life there in that familiar space. Her rooms were my rooms.

I didn't want to be alone. I took a short drive and sat for a while in the morning in my parents' kitchen. Members of my family came and went, everyone strangely insular, upbeat, almost professional in what had now, almost subtly, become a vigil. My daughter, two-and-a-half, played happily, oblivious to these occurrences which were effectively writing page one in the story of her life. I tried to eat something. My mother-in-law came, having just stopped to see Louise. She was upright, composed, heartsick. It speaks directly to the horror of what was happening to Louise that neither her mother nor her husband could any longer bear to watch.

We spoke little of what was really happening. We would

speak later. At such a time one's own pain is enough, and more. There can be no sharing. The death grip divides, and stifles. We packed up my daughter's things. I didn't want to let her out of my sight. I held her for a long time before they left. Others filtered off. Now it was just my father and I in the house. I put on a sweater and got into bed, waiting for a phone call, listening for footsteps.

I have a girlfriend now. She's a little younger than me, sweet, easy to be with. She came into my life suddenly, like an angel almost. At that time for me the world was aflutter with angels. Several months after Louise died I poked my head out through a cloud of grief, breathed in the blue snap of an April breeze, and decided that I feared nothing. I had been through the worst and was still here, as though I had returned from years of battle on some distant, harrowing front. I had been through something cataclysmic, hellish, almost surreal. And although I had been damaged, and had lost a dear friend, I was glad it was over. I found myself, but only briefly—caught up as I was in the grip of a process that I was only beginning to understand—quite unexpectedly ecstatic to be alive, and to be home. I found that there is a certain freedom to being destroyed. It's almost like being reborn. You're a child again. People care for you.

When I met my girlfriend—we can call her Annie—she just seemed to shine for me somehow. I have never been any great ladies' man to say the least—my wife was the only woman I had ever seriously dated, and in many ways she had chosen me—but Annie I pursued fearlessly. After checking with a couple of friends, asking permission almost, I wooed her with the intensity of a prophet. To my astonishment she responded, and before long we were together.

That was less than six months after my wife died. If that seems too soon, it's because it probably was. But I did not feel the need to explain myself then, nor do I have any regrets now, two years later. I was just raw and exposed—ripped open wide as a new day and all the light pouring in. I needed someone to help me catch my balance. In truth I might have fallen for anyone—it was only dumb luck that I happened upon one so kind. And I don't take Annie for granted. Anyone else would have run off long ago.

It now seems possible that the one, and true, and enduring love of my remaining days will be one who goes by many names: Sweet Pea, Miss Baba-Loo, Baby Cakes, Peanut, Goose, Petunia, Baby Girl, Punkin', Her Royal Highness the Queen—my daughter, my reason for being on most days, this child of mine, Robin.

She is nearly five now, and although she looks like me she is her mother to the very merry marrow of her bones: beautiful, loquacious, dreamy, funny, charming, temperamental, and demanding. Further, she is adored by many, including me. And further still, as she has stated on many occasions, she wants to marry me.

Of course I said yes.

Now it is winter and snow is falling. More than a foot of snow last weekend and more falling. Beautiful, keep snowing. Bury me.

I'm finding this out: I'm tired. I took a nap this morning. *A morning nap!* I'm sleeping. Sleep started coming on and I just wrapped up in a big wool blanket and let it fall all over me—ten in the morning. I'm pulling it all in now, shutting down. Grief is a relentless and futile emotion. It's been pounding on me, you see. I'm beaten up. I give! It has been more than two years since Louise disappeared. Too long to be taking that kind of beating without rest. I'm taking some time. On my board at work I wrote: "Hibernating—see you in spring."

A winter in my cave, dreaming. Things will be better if I do this, sure. Do it through sleeping and waking, by degree. Louise sleeps, too. It is the only place we can be together now, in our sleeping.

My darling wife, two years in her sleeping now. Two years: an arbitrary span of time meaning forever or nothing. And yet I fall back further still—five years, ten years, even more—to find the other end of this thread, which began in passion and in waking and through its long and strange and futile unraveling ended here, in sleeping and forgetting.

It is a difficult road. But I am safe now and up to the journey back—back to a time before I slipped into this role of single father which still seems to fit like somebody else's suit, still feels as though it is somebody else's life entirely. Back before it was just me and Robin holding hands on a winter's morning leading a congregation of mourners into an empty church. Before the bone marrow transplant and all the rounds of chemotherapy and the dizzying medical details I never really attempted to understand, still struggle to forget. Back before breast cancer rudely wedged itself into our lives even as we held the door open to welcome Robin in.

I want to go back to the beginning of this road, to see that it is all still there. I want to go over and over it again. I want to burn it in, keep it, give it to my daughter sometime. We go forward into our lives and Robin and I will be fine but we can keep this for ourselves. Louise will forever be real here on this stretch of road that we keep.

I want always for Robin to see that at the beginning of this road there is a woman who was young and complex and beautiful whom I loved. Louise was not perfect. I was so young myself and in many ways she toyed with me. She had been in one or two longer relationships by the time we met, and I was really still just a boy, clumsy and awkward with women, possessing perhaps some potential but with absolutely no idea what to do with it. Where she had become wary I was simply green. I always felt we redeemed one another.

Louise could drive me half-mad, but never tired, never bored. She was like fine porcelain: beautiful and proud, but also fragile, to be handled carefully. She knew she was good, she loved herself, and so I knew I could always love her too, knew she could always dazzle me because she wanted to, it was in her power. Her face was like big water, always changing, shimmering almost like a movie of her life: back and forth, the roles she played—a little girl, a mother, a daughter and a woman—sometimes all of them at once.

She had the eyes of a cat, deep-set, slate-blue and serene, sensuous, and they commanded the attention of whatever they were fixing on. I miss those eyes, the way they fixed on me. She really cared for her skin, kept it soft and white, smooth and expressive, sensitive—every thought, every feeling, even the gentlest inclination rippling telltale across her face—like wind across water, her hair blowing like sea-grass. Her mouth could tell me her mind by the way it turned. And those lips—full as ripe plums. They were mine. That kiss was *mine*.

Several years ago she invited me to a party at the flat she shared with a friend. I was but twenty-four. We were only acquaintances at the time, though already—as we soon discovered and laughed about—there had formed a private, mutual admiration society. The party was dense with revelers and at full tilt when I got there. It was December, around the holidays, and the rooms were glowing with cheer and the soft light of candles, candles floating in the bathtub even. Music and laughter and voices floated on the air like great, graceful birds.

I had to drive across town to get there and had gotten lost, and so I was late. I met her roommate first in the long, narrow hallway ("You must be Dave!" she exclaimed, half-tipsy on holiday wine as I walked up, and my confidence was bolstered by the fact that I had been talked about and expected.) Self-conscious and in need of some purpose, I made for the crowded kitchen to put a bottle into the refrigerator and to see if there was even a soul there that I could recognize. As I passed through the dining room I spotted Louise in a far corner looking beautiful and sexy as hell in a black leather skirt and black sweater, talking intently with someone and not even noticing me. In the kitchen I jostled awkwardly to get the refrigerator door open amid the throngs and when I stood up to turn around I suddenly found myself cheerfully embraced by a lovely, half-tight woman who threw her arms around me, kissed me hard on the cheek and exclaimed, "You came!"

Louise had spotted me after all. That was a kiss I have never forgotten. I can still *feel* it, do you know? So much exploded from that kiss, as though it opened a door into my very soul: like a portal, so much bursting forth. That kiss sounded the beginning of something, some chapter or stage of fate, and through the door came rushes and waves and trickles of a story that still has not stopped. Louise was so resolved, the way she kissed me then. It was almost as though she chose me there. Almost as though she knew.

Time flows through us and much is forgotten, but some things you can never forget. The past has a way of disappearing as it recedes—like the tide moving out—but it's strange how as the water recedes some things remain firm, hard and certain and unmovable as stones etched fast upon the shore. Those interminable rocks—those are the things we hold onto forever. Our lives flow through us and become stone.

2

.

I was first introduced to my daughter through a television screen, on an ultrasound machine. She was seven months in utero and all the parts were in place—or so they appeared to my untrained eye as the pictures flickered and shifted with the movement of the camera across Louise's belly. The nurse interpreted for us: "There's the head, see? And this is a leg, kind of curled up under its little butt."

Then briefly another image flashed, and I thought to myself what is that *there?* That narrow, hollow place coursing up through the center of his torso, where his little Mr. Johnson is supposed to be? Hmmmm....

I said nothing about this to Louise, because she wanted to be surprised, and I really only half-admitted it to myself. I was convinced we were going to have a boy, and perhaps everything that was male and prideful within me was telling me I was supposed to *want* a boy. But I had seen what I had seen and I was immediately and unexpectedly relieved. Apparently I had been secretly wishing for a girl all along. We even had her name all picked out in case— Robin—a lovely, simple name for a girl born in springtime, and in my imaginings throughout the rest of that day and into the night this child, this creature, had suddenly begun to emerge as something possible, definite, *real*. There was going to be a little girl in the world, and she was going to call me Daddy.

But it was just a few nights later, on a Sunday evening after we had gone to bed, in those fitful and dark hours—that lonely, anxious, strangely dreadful chasm of time between the end of something and the dawn of something new—that another visitor, this one horrible and stealthy, was also born into our lives.

Louise would later tell me that she had been half-aware of the strange mass in her breast for some time. But it was not until she had seen that ultrasound of our baby, had absorbed the reality that this child was indeed coming, and soon, and that it was a healthy baby, *her* baby—only then could she even confront the possibility of this other thing... that it surely wasn't...that it was obviously *not*...only then could she even acknowledge that this dark, forbidding curtain was even there, much less wish to confront it, to take a peek behind it. If only to confirm that this was something easily explainable and related to all the other wild changes occurring in her body now, and that her fears were simply the product of a very understandable paranoia that must confront all women when they are pregnant with their first child.

The following morning Louise mentioned it to me in passing almost, told me she was going to go see her doctor if only to give her some peace of mind about it. I don't remember being overly concerned. This whole pregnancy had been an education to me, all the changes in her body, both minor and major, all their ramifications—I had probably grown a little weary of it after a while, perhaps even a little queasy to be honest. The human body—that it works is enough for me, I guess—the chemistry and biology I take on faith, file it all away in a large folder in my head labeled "The General Mystery."

With my head in those vapors of mystery the call found me oblivious and off-guard later that afternoon. Louise was frantic. Her doctor was concerned, she said, *quite* concerned about the size and location of this mass. It was probably nothing, but to be certain she was sending Louise immediately to another doctor that very afternoon for a biopsy.

And so it was that on that day, which found us waking to dreams and possibilities and new life, that we were introduced to nightmares, and realities, and death. What would follow was a process so humiliating and methodical in its destruction and so predictable in its evasiveness, that I suffer to even recall many of the more mundane particulars—doctor visits, medical procedures and terms, surgeries both minor and major, setbacks and treatments and new clinical studies that only briefly offered some hope.

Details I long ago dropped and ran from. And despite all my attempts at forgetting—it is a willful forgetting, I *work* at it, because to remember gives it power—I am still left with bitter memories of Louise in her suffering, and with such an admiration for her courage in the fight that to know I've lost her hurts more.

So she sleeps. I can only hope that it's true what they say—that we are purified through suffering—and that she is somehow, somewhere pure, complete, and whole now in her sleeping. Perhaps someday I can find that too and we can lie together again.

Events quickly swept us up following that bitter February day. Two weeks later I found myself sitting inexplicably all alone in a hospital waiting room, waiting for the doctor to come with news of the surgery. There had been two biopsies with conflicting results, so they decided to remove the tumor to be absolutely sure, and I was now waiting for her to come out of that surgery, and for the doctor to come with news of what he'd found. I was still hopeful—certain almost—that things were going to be fine.

But as I waited the doubts and fears began to simply overcome me. I had been trying to play it cool—to this day I am mystified at my decision to endure that morning alone—and yet my body seemed to absolutely take over as if to awaken me to the possibility that a big blow was coming and I had better be prepared. A mild panic came over me as I sat there, all alone in that sunny, comfortable room. I got up and walked. I looked out the window and sat down again, my beloved stoicism having abandoned me, and *Oh my God for somebody to talk to.*

That was where they found me, the two surgeons in their green hospital scrubs, when they came finally. I stood to greet them. The one was grave and thoughtful and silent, the other grave and direct and definitive as he approached and shook my hand and said, even before sitting down, "Mr. Collins, we have a breast cancer."

The power of the words alone must have knocked me to my seat, because the next thing I recall is that I had sat down, looked around the empty room, whistled through my teeth and said simply "Goddamn."

Aside from the obvious emotional blow to us both, Louise and I also found ourselves caught up very suddenly in a complex medical situation that seemed to take on a life of its own. Louise was *pregnant*. Treatments had to begin soon. Calls were made between doctors. We decided (or it was decided for us) that Louise would carry her baby to eight months before labor was induced. Then they would start going after the cancer.

I think of Robin there, in her silent, black, watery world. Could she feel all of this tumult? Or was it like a storm raging on the surface while she floated peacefully, far below? Was she even Robin, *our Robin*, or did her person come later, after she was born?

So strange and ironic—mythical almost—to think that this beautiful, miraculous gift of a new child was roaring into our lives even as this other terror was circling us. Robin literally passed into this world through the eye of a needle. We did not know it then, but the door was closing on the chance that we would ever have another child. Had the cancer struck sooner, before Louise had become pregnant, it is likely that Robin would have never been conceived: we would not find this out until later—another heavy blow in a barrage of many—but the chemotherapy treatments were certain to bring on menopause. And if Louise had only been a few months along in her pregnancy an abortion might have been necessary, so the treatments could commence sooner. But the baby was developed enough at seven months to withstand the surgeries and stress. Her little lungs were still growing, but she should be strong enough, the doctors hoped, to breathe on her own when the time came.

About a week after they found the cancer, Louise had to have another surgery—this one more invasive. They cut lymph nodes out from under her arm. The nodes would tell her doctors more about the progress of the disease. This time there was general anesthesia, possibly a danger to the baby—more worries. Five o'clock in the morning and back at the hospital. Louise smiled and hummed in the pre-op room when the drugs hit. I was holding her hand, my guts aching, knives slicing up under my arms: sympathetic pain. A priest came and held our hands and said a prayer.

Soon they were coming to take her in. She was frightened, but brave. I smiled for her, laughed at the silly nonsense she was talking as the drugs took hold, but I could feel the crying coming on. Louise tapped her hands upon her belly and said something to the baby. I saw a woman—a young, pretty black woman—standing by and watching us intently with a folded-up church missile in her hand, stalwart and proud, like a sentry, her lips moving as though in a silent prayer. Even in my distraction it struck me as strange. I had the thought: *an angel.* I had never suffered like this before and already I was seeing things, visions and little miracles, deft and commonplace, sightings easily missed by most people but visible to me now, almost as though under pressure certain things are forced into relief.

When they finally wheeled her into the operating room I picked up my paper and jacket and went to look for my little restroom around the corner. Nobody in there—good. I was just going to make it. I locked the door, leaned on the sink and watched in the mirror as the sobs broke across my face. Sobs of a little boy. I had not cried like this since childhood and now it was coming on every day, convulsively, breaking up and over me in waves when I could not hold it down any longer. She had been in the hospital for more than a week. Every day I'd sit with her, holding her hand, holding it down and staying with her as long as I could, until it could not be denied any longer. I'd get up to go…

Not yet. Hold it, hold it. You've got to be bigger than this. Hold onto it now. Don't let her see it. You'll get your spot. Okay say goodbye and hold onto it. Hold her tight and give her a kiss and stay with it...

"Okay, good night sweetie," I'd say finally. "Sleep well. It's going to be alright. You know that. Try to get some sleep. I love you. I'll be back in the morning. Yes. Good night. I love you. Good night."

Good. Now keep holding it. Smile and wave. Blow a kiss and you're out. Down the hall. Nobody in here. Okay. Let it go. Alright, alright, alright...

Now I am two people. There is me here crying, and me here watching me crying. Strange to be here outside myself. Listen to him. He is but a boy. Haven't heard his voice since he was seven years old and fell off his bike. The handlebars were stripped. He went flying over them and landed on his chin. A sunny summer's morning on the old lane...

Look at him. He is a man but he carries the boy with him, still. Why two of us? Look at his face. He's having it rough—needs sleep. He hasn't the guts for this. Oh yeah? You try me. That's it. That's a little better. Out the door and down the hall. Eyes red like you've been crying but who cares. Let them look. I'm going home now. Is this the way it's going to be? Alone like this?

I had found my places around the hospital—restrooms, empty hallways, the sidewalk out front—for my little private breakdowns. I would sit with her in her room and watch television as she slept. Sometimes we would watch together—game shows, sitcoms, soap operas—the comfort food of television. Or, we would catch up on all the goings on around the house, gossip about friends and work, talk about our baby and how we were going to fit this new creature into our lives. We didn't talk about her disease much, both trying to be strong for the other. Mostly I tried to pump her up, like a coach before a big game, the only language I could find that seemed to fit.

"Baby, you are going to kick this thing's *ass*," I'd say, quietly, but with intent. I would hold her hand, lie down in the hospital bed beside her. "Do you know how tough you are? You're *too* tough, too strong."

I would try to convince myself even: "And anyway they got it in time—it's going to be alright, sweetheart. It's going to be fine."

It seemed to pick her up. Her cheeks flushed warmly as she sat up in bed and crowed bravely for me—but still so frightened, I could see, like a child: my heart breaking *(hold it, hold it now)*. She would perk up and brighten at the thought of having this *behind* her soon, would talk about how the experience had given her a new perspective, a wake-up call: she actually felt lucky in a way, because they got the cancer in time. It could have been worse, she'd say, and I believed it too. Both of us believed it as naturally as breathing.

In the second operation they dug twenty lymph nodes— like twenty tiny pebbles—out of her armpit. What were they *looking* for? Our fate? They may as well be reading tea leaves. And what do they reveal, Doctor? Oh, we have to wait? *Ten days?!* Ten days to wait for a pathology report in a manila envelope to tell us the course of our future—the course of her *life*—the sheer weight of it, words on a piece of paper, the paper sealed in an envelope and picked up by a delivery boy, the boy tossing the envelope on the front seat of his car as he drives across town listening to country music and eating a sandwich. Our destiny in that report, taking its time.

3

Already late morning and still below zero. I have accomplished nothing today and yet I'm tired and want to sleep, only sleep. Robin and I had a huge row again this morning and I want only to sleep the day away and then pick her up early from her preschool and hold her and kiss her and tell her I'm sorry. I'm feeling silly and a little ashamed at my fury of this morning but at the time it was real. I think I'm in control but I really have no idea. Absolutely none. I tell myself you are not really in control unless you are willing to lose it occasionally.

It was the royal underwear that set me off, finally. Her Worshipfulness did not want to wear the clean, white, neatly folded underpants I set out for her this morning. She wanted to wear the purple *Barbie* underpants she's been wearing now for nearly a week, and I was having nothing more of it. Typically, this confrontation occurred two minutes before we had to be out the door, when my willingness to stand my ground was being overcome by my obsession with staying on schedule. This child is a wily animal in that way—picking her spots with the accuracy of a surgeon—but this morning I was ready for her. We would go as far and get as dirty as she wanted to, but I was not going to give in.

"No, you may *not* wear the purple underpants today," I said. "You can put on the clean underpants I put out for you. And that's *it*. That's all there is to it."

I laid it down just like that, strong and firm. You have to be firm with children. If we cave in here—with underpants —then what is next? Drugs? Gunplay? No, we must stand on this ground, dig in. If we lose here, we lose everywhere. In a way, it all comes down to underpants and standing firm in our resolve to wear the *proper* underpants goddamnit.

And to further illustrate, see how quickly it can escalate: suddenly it was not just underpants, but the jeans as well. She dropped the underpants issue for a moment and went on to point out that she did not want to wear the *blue* jeans. She wanted to wear the *green* jeans, and by the tone of her voice I guessed I was some blathering moron for not realizing this. This despite the fact, which I so patiently pointed out while tapping my foot heavily now by the back steps, that the green jeans obviously did not go with the little lacey-pink-thing shirt she was wearing. We would have to change the shirt, too, and we did not have time for that now because it was now TIME TO GO WE'RE LATE WHAT POSSIBLE DIFFERENCE COULD IT MAKE?!

To this she responded by going back to the laundry pile to retrieve the soiled purple underpants, running into her room, slamming the door, and hollering out to me, through sobs and much wailing: "All I want to do is wear the purple underpants just *One. More. Day!* I *never* get to wear the purple underpants! Ever!"

Oh baby, now it was on. Alright, we're going to the mat on this one, sweetie pie! We are going to learn the meaning of the word "No" today.

I crashed through her door: "You don't slam the door on me like that!" I hollered. "I said no! Do you know what that means? It means no! NO! NO! NO! We don't just wear our dirty underwear for weeks and weeks around here— especially, and here is the important point—especially when I say NO!"

She could see I meant business this time, and though she whined and paced about the room for a few moments, longingly, desperately clinging to her prized, soon-to-be abandoned purple underpants with the *Barbie* across the front, she finally *ambled* over and began to put on the clean underwear. Alright, I thought, that round goes to me. "If you want to wear the green pants, fine," I offered as a consolation (fatal weakness, you fool!). "It will look silly, but fine. Just get them on, so we can go. We're *late*. Again this morning we're late because of *all this screwing around* at the last minute."

But of course, and probably due in large part to that momentary softening in my position, there was more. Robin had already eaten a full, hot breakfast, but she had asked for a little bowl of dry cereal to snack on while she was watching television afterwards, and for the car ride to her school—all in accordance with her very carefully developed routine. But by the time we were ready to leave, she had finished most of what I had given her and asked if I could pour a little more cereal in her bowl, a different kind of cereal this time, though, of course—always with the stipulations and caveats, always with the fine-tuning with my child. "Fine. I'll get you a little more. Just get ready so we can go."

So I poured the *new* cereal right on top of the *old* cereal (how thoughtless, how completely foolish), helped her into her boots and coat and hat and mittens, trying, trying,

trying to maintain my patience. I could hear the car engine running out on the driveway, the car engine I had started fifteen minutes earlier in hopes of a smooth departure. I handed her the bowl of cereal, opened the door and gently, firmly, ushered her out.

She stopped: "But *Daaaddyyyyy*...(oh God, here it comes again)...you were supposed to empty the other cereal out before you poured the new cereal in! Now they're all mixed up *together*. I can't eat *this!*"

And now that last layer of skin has finally worn away. Now I am in full explosion, roiling with a complex cocktail of emotions that includes impatience, self-pity, and utter vexation, intense feelings even on their own, but now made all the more lethal by their combined force, working together as a unit to attack and brutally overcome whatever self-control I have left. I snatch the bowl away and fling it back into the house, cereal scattering everywhere. I pick up the child in one arm and stomp out onto the driveway, wondering briefly if the neighbors are watching, if they can see me now or have been witness to the many other occasions when this exact scenario has played itself out here, on my driveway, at ten after eight in the morning, with the car engine running, the child wailing, the lunatic stomping and slamming and cursing and finally backing down the driveway with a squeal of rubber at a hundred miles an hour. I wonder, and yet I strangely don't care, because they do not know, could not know, how my morning had started with the bravest intentions and strong determination to remain patient and calm, and yet had somehow, as on so many other mornings, deteriorated to what they were witnessing now—the brief, thirty-second, final and climactic scene of a much longer and more complex drama than they could possibly imagine—played out in the bleak, early morning half-light, featuring a poor, sweet, motherless child and her asshole father who, quite clearly, abuses her.

Now we have tapped into the deepest well—all the bitterness and frustration, the anger—bubbling up and out, and I am really powerless to stop it, wouldn't stop it if I could really (it simply *must* come out), and I am again aware that I have become two people, one of us now a raging lunatic in full harangue, the other calm, more removed, observing, not even trying to stop the lunatic guy because he knows that once the fire is lit it must burn until all the fuel has been consumed.

And really the raging lunatic is making some excellent points as he steers the car through the neighborhood streets on the way to school, the bass line of his voice being finely complemented by the rising and falling melody of the child's sobs emanating from the back seat:

"Robin!" I holler (I am *hollering* now), "I am getting awfully tired of having to go through this little charade every morning…every morning you pull this crap: you don't like your underwear, you don't like your shoes, you don't like your breakfast. Every morning at the last minute until I lose my temper, and it just *doesn't* have to be that way!"

And on and on he goes. Throughout all this, the calm voice is saying, "You sound like your father and one of his lectures from years ago—thorough, reasoned, loud, and laced with disappointment and disgust. Only this child is not even *five*. You sound like an idiot. Look at the poor kid back there, wailing and calling for her mother. And you, the absolute center of her universe, sitting here laying this big *trip* on her. Ridiculous."

I honestly don't know which voice is right. The crazy guy is out of control, clearly, and all that anger and bile is no good, but he's essentially right. He has to stick up for himself somehow. It's true, the child does not listen, often will not follow instructions until the lunatic comes out to really drive the point home, forcefully, with some steam behind it. I wonder if other parents are driven so mad-crazy, or if they're able to get the point across in other ways.

Be firm, but gentle—that's what all the parenting books and magazine articles I don't have time to read seem to say. But in the world I inhabit it is pretty tough to maintain that kind of composure, that steadiness. I usually find myself letting things slide until I can't stand it anymore. Firm, but gentle? I don't know. I think the proper way to describe my style would be: permissive, but vindictive.

I know that a great deal of this anger is coming from some other source—from my feelings of being saddled with handling this whole job by myself, no backup, no helper—though it would be utterly unfair, even irresponsible, to lay any of that on Robin. It's just a tough, tough spot—being a single parent. All that pressure: it's more than double, more like triple or quadruple the pressure that a normal parent feels because you never have that *out*, that tag-team partner who can come in and take over when you've simply had enough. Consequently there are many, many times when you find yourself in there dealing with a situation that you really shouldn't be dealing with at all, in the state of mind you're in. You should be off taking a walk or running errands, cooling down, but instead you have to be there because there is no one else. So you lose control, right there in the heat of it: you blow it right in front of your kid. And you hate yourself for presenting that kind of example to your own child. You know she's watching and learning. Some of your worst qualities laid bare for the taking, the smooth transfer of your ugliest side to the next generation happening as you watch, and you are momentarily powerless to stop it.

Louise comes to me still, sometimes. She's here now. We've spoken. She sends me geese: little postcards I call them—*see my geese in their vees on the sky through the trees.* The beating of wings, a glance up at the gunmetal sky, and there she is: *did you see my geese?* Her voice mischievous and happy. Sometimes my daughter is in my arms when they fly over, but I haven't shared this with her yet. Maybe soon, though. A little at a time with her. She has her whole life to figure this out. Anyway, she's closer to her mother than I'll ever be. Almost the same person, really, it's that close. It would be spooky if it weren't so delightful. That little sparkle, the jingle in her eyes: sometimes I think they're really playing with me, the two of them, and that it's all a game and we're all together, always, and life is just a pool in time, we dip in we dip out, all to amuse ourselves, because we're all immortal and eternity is, despite its obvious benefits, quite frankly, boring.

She is sometimes near and others far. Always she comes, though, when I call. She's off flying around. I would be too. I would go far, far back into primordial time. I would want to see the earth before people, before dinosaurs even, or any living thing. Way back when it was just empty desolate time. Waves crashing ashore, volcanoes boiling: a hurricane that no one saw. I would want to simply *feel* all that time, the great hollow stretch of it, and then realize I was outside of it, like a god peering into a raindrop and nothing around me but nothing, everything. Not lonely, not at all.

Our daughter was born on a cold afternoon in late March. They had given Louise a month to recover from the surgery and now, eight months pregnant, she was going to have induced labor. The tumor in her breast was gone, the lymph nodes looked good—no sign that the cancer had spread—and now the plan was to get that baby.

After the baby was born there would be the whole ordeal of chemotherapy, but for now we were trying to push all of that away so we could celebrate the birth of our first child. It was an intense, stormy time, but it was not without its moments of calm, of beauty and hope. Despite our obvious anxieties, we were also excited—things were happening, but we were young and resilient and we could handle it. Maybe it could be done. Actually, *hell yes*, we knew it could be done. Everything else collapsing away and only this and it was going to get done.

Now the baby. Some question about her breathing—could she breathe on her own?—the lungs develop late in the pregnancy and we were cutting the pregnancy short. Otherwise the baby looked to be strong and healthy, the doctor said. She looked good in there (not certain it was a she, but thinking it was, both of us).

We had a nice dinner at home, just Louise and me. Louise had a little wine: I had a lot of wine. We would be going to the hospital later that evening, to check Louise in, get her to bed, so she could have the baby the next day—everything right on schedule, like having an appointment to have a baby. I have a photograph of her from that night, standing sideways in our living room and smiling for the camera, her arms about her waist rocking the baby. Her hair was never that long again.

We were seizing that moment of calm, savoring it. We got some music going. I was sky-high and a little tight. She was nervous and giddy. We drove to the hospital, music pumping, me trying to get her ready, her laughing at me like I was nuts, both of us singing along to the music. Later, I went home to sleep. Her call woke me up early the next morning. "Sweetheart, things are starting to *happen*. I thought you might want to get over here."

Same hospital as before, different floor. A far more cheerful place. In the early morning they hooked up an IV drip to start the contractions. It took a while, so we waited. We had a private room, spacious and modern with a window. I pulled open all the blinds: outside a typical early spring morning, raw, cold and damp, huge snowflakes floating down. The nurse came in and out to check the monitors, capable and reassuring, like your new best friend. I took a walk down the corridor and saw her doctor sitting in a comfortable chair at the nurses' station. She was knitting a sweater, waiting for the action to start, like a goddess—so calm, the one who was guiding us through this. How could it not be alright?

As the day moved on the contractions started, lightly at first. We watched television, listened to music, giggled in wonderment at the thought: our baby coming. More contractions, now painful, the water breaking in the late afternoon light.

"*Whooooosh!*" Louise explained when the torrent rained. I watched from the window, wobbly with the odor of it. Now things were picking up. The contractions were more frequent, more painful. We're getting close·now, the doctor coming in every few minutes: "It's almost time for the baby, Louise—do you even *want* the epidural?" Oh you'd better believe she does. Moaning in pain under her mask. Me holding her hand saying something about a mountain— climbing the mountain *(idiot!)*—and her telling me: "Honey,

I really need you to shut up now! *And where is that goddamn epidural!"*

Finally they anaesthetize her spine, her body relaxes, and suddenly the baby is near. Me holding her hand but most definitely out of the fray. Not interested in the finer points of biology, doctor, thank you. Certain things can remain a mystery.

"Dad, would you like to see the crown of the baby's head?" Well, okay…*oh, oh, oh*…that's enough: was that a wobble? You wobbled! I didn't really need to see that. A little brown hairy crown, buried in there like a potato in the garden. Some sort of creature rising up from the primordial ooze. What in God's name is that thing in there? Where did it *come* from?

The floor moved a little beneath my feet and there was a pause, much screaming, a whirl of action. Suddenly a brown, wrinkled doll was dangling upside down before me, a look of surprised irritation upon her face as though she was being roused out of a thousand-year sleep. "Louise," the doctor said, "you have a beautiful baby girl!"

Totally in the moment, Louise cheered and cried. Whereas I was exactly three seconds *behind* the moment, stunned, standing there a little to the side, watching myself watching, finally getting it. Oh, it's a *baby*! A little girl. But…well…why does she look so pissed off?

At times, with all that has occurred since, that day seems an eternity ago—but at others, like today, as I find myself worrying again about my daughter's future—it seems as though her life has exploded from that moment and I have been little more than a bystander in my attempts to guide her. Things are happening so quickly that when I get a moment to reflect a near panic sets in. Do I actually have a plan for her, or are things just *happening* to us? I am normally confident and pretty easygoing about this, but occasionally doubts arise and I suddenly wonder if I have any clue as to what I'm doing. And this time it is no small thing I'm fretting over. You see, very soon I must choose a kindergarten for Robin.

It sounds silly, but this is actually a big decision for me. I suppose I should be grateful that I have a choice. Many people do not have the ways or means, or even the imagination, to do anything other than march their kid down to the local public school, shake hands with the teacher, wish them luck, and be done with it. I'm fortunate that our small community here does have good schools. There is an elementary school two blocks away. I took Robin over there one afternoon. We met the principal, who took us on a tour of the classrooms and the library and the gym. It seemed fine. We were both excited. I can easily close my eyes and see myself helping Robin into her raincoat and boots on a foggy autumn morning, see us walking hand-in-hand and waving to the crossing guard on the way to her little neighborhood school.

Or I can choose to send her to another school across town, where the real estate is a little pricier, the parents a little older and wealthier and also probably a bit more *involved* in that sometimes overbearing way that very successful parents can be. It is supposed to be a good school, but I know that kind of an environment would require a bit of an adjustment for both Robin and me. I've heard a few stories about that school, accounts of nervous, overly protective mothers and fathers literally hovering over their children as they make their way from class to class. All the precious little darlings.

Or perhaps this is all some class warfare of my own devising. Louise always accused me of being a "retro-snob" as she called it. Perhaps I'm being overly protective myself when I wonder whether in time some of her classmates might begin to look down upon Robin. What if they try to make her feel like she's an outsider, or inferior. Maybe they'll tease her. Perhaps she'll come home from school crying one day because she doesn't have all the latest, most expensive clothes like the kids in her class. Maybe she'll start to envy them their big houses, or their summer homes. I actually lie awake at night worrying about these things.

I could also choose to send Robin to a Catholic school. I went to Catholic school all the way through high school and it didn't screw me up too badly. When my mother and father were getting me ready for elementary school, I don't think there was a second thought about where I was headed. St. Michael's was practically in my backyard. All I had to do was walk out the back door and follow the little path through the woods to the schoolyard—a path worn through by the footsteps of my six older brothers and sisters who preceded me there.

I doubt my parents fretted over the decision the way I'm fretting now, which may or may not be good. I didn't get off to such a good start. My first-grade teacher was a stern amazon of a nun who had me so petrified I begged to be sent to public school. And although I recovered from that first year and went on to do well at St. Michael's, maybe some other school would have been better for me.

I don't know how Robin would respond to the more regimented Catholic school experience. I'm sure today the schools have changed quite a bit, become more enlightened and modern. And they do get results. Isn't that the most important thing? But having been through all that, and knowing my daughter the way I do, I guess I envision something different for her. Robin has her own mind, is very free-spirited, and if anyone tries to plant her in a chair for six hours and spoon-feed her she'll run in the other direction. They'll never catch her.

Still, the religious aspect of a Catholic school is something to consider, if only to get her thinking along those lines. Robin loves Bible stories. So much of what Jesus taught—if you can separate it from the grotesque misrepresentations found everywhere—is really very simple and beautiful and universal. And it need not be divisive, to learn a faith. What Jesus taught is not much different from what the founders of Judaism, Buddhism, or Islam taught, nor from what thousands of other anonymous sages and scholars, even ordinary men and women, have discovered on their own throughout time and across cultures. It seems valuable to at least get a start on thinking about these things, to learn at a young age that your actions have consequences, that there is a right and wrong way to treat your fellow humans, that there is an imperative to be kind to all the creatures of the earth even, and to the earth itself. It's okay to learn guilt as well—to know some moral standard and to feel bad when you violate it. I would like for Robin to at least be exposed to these ideas. Later, when she is an adult and has thought all of this through, she can choose her own way. But at least it will be a careful choice.

Maybe there is yet another way. I'm going to look further. There are new schools, new approaches now. And Robin does seem to be a bit *different*. She is very imaginative, seems to get far away sometimes in her play. She can play happily among ten or twelve other children without actually including them in the world she's inhabiting. And she pleases herself: she apparently has no need to prove to me that she can write her name or add numbers or read a few words. I don't mind. She'll get it. She's a little girl—I want her to play. Robin has such a talent for words and sounds that she'll learn to read by accident. What is more important is that she knows what she likes and how to get it. That is something she can't learn when she's older. So many adults I know are driven by a need to please others and rarely feel like they do. Robin knows what makes her happy and knows enough to insist upon it—if she can hang onto that quality her education is ninety percent complete. The rest is just details.

Whatever I choose, I want to be extra careful to get what's best for her—the absolute best I can give her—because I know what she's missing out on. Louise was to be Robin's teacher. There are so many things, girl things and also other things, that I can't provide. Louise was supposed to be Robin's guide through her girlhood and beyond, was to provide the example of the woman that Robin will one day become.

There are so many practical things—the simple skills and tricks and trappings of girls—like sewing with needle and thread, arranging and caring for her little dolls and jewelry, painting toenails, or drying and pressing flowers. My inadequacies in these areas are blatantly obvious. I notice them at Christmas when I try to decorate our house for the holidays, and especially while wrapping gifts. Louise could wrap a package so creatively, a different way each time using colorful papers, old photographs, ribbons and paints, that the wrapping itself became far more beautiful than whatever was inside. She saw colors that I never saw: a thing was not red, it was brick—not blue, but azure. She simply had taste, an eye for detail, for discerning the fineness of something, and the confidence and vocabulary for sizing it up and choosing. These are qualities that she absorbed from her own mother, I'm certain, over time, simply by observing her and admiring her—worshipping her even.

It saddens me for Robin that she will not have the privilege of watching her mother in the plain actions of everyday living. She won't be able to watch her deliberating and fussing in some little shop as she tries to pick out the perfect stationery, won't lie on our bed, chin propped in her hands dreamily, watching Louise primp before a mirror in her lingerie before a big evening out, won't taggle along behind as her mother strolls with awed pleasure through an art gallery before arriving at one particular piece that dazzles her—that she simply must have.

This was to be Robin's truest education, as it should be for any little girl. They learn from the people whom they naturally adore. But it is the harsh fact—and I must face it for Robin even if she cannot—that all of that is gone now. Lost. There is just nothingness in that space where her mother had been, and as Robin grows I can see her becoming more conscious of that emptiness. She can feel the pull of it, for it has a pull, a force that strangely brings both comfort and pain—comfort in that her absence is at least proof that she once was, pain in that she is absent at all.

Robin will have to learn to live with this fact. This is her mother. Louise is there and not there. She is gravity now, with all the pull and power of a collapsing star. All that is drawn to her disappears.

But while that void is vast and powerful, it is my responsibility—my mission now, as I've come to recognize—to make sure that Robin does not fixate on that emptiness. That space where her mother was, that portal to who knows where, is not for the living. Louise is words and stories and photographs now. We will remember—we will never forget. But while the space she once occupied is now empty, there is new territory to be explored, virgin territory, a whole universe of it and more every day. It is exploding in every direction. Robin must be guided out toward that. She is alive. That is what living is for. The place where Louise has gone—we will all go there eventually. I will go there, and then Robin too, and we will be a family again. But for now, and here, we may as well go out and carve some territory, raise some hell and dust and vibrations.

4

When I think back over her sickness, even all this time later, it is still with such fresh regret and horror that my mind can only skim past, almost like a scientist would fly over the sight of a nuclear accident—hastily, from a safe altitude, in his protective suit. I do not like to go there often. I've tried to bury much of it. I think of Louise almost constantly, but not in that way when I can help it—not in her falling. Still, things come up—conversations, smells, songs on the radio—that trigger memories of those bad times. They come up and I see them and bury them again and move on. You have got to keep moving. Those horrors have a pull, too. They can bring you down.

But when I must, when it is unavoidable, I put on my yellow suit and my mask and my rubber boots, and I get in my airplane and I fly over, being careful not to fly too close to the ground. Despite the danger, I am passive and without panic in my flying—she is not down there anymore. She is gone now, and safe. I don't need to think anymore of some desperate attempt at a rescue, don't need to sense that futility ever again, nor the inadequacy of knowing I can do nothing. It is a lonely, quiet memoryscape I see below. Still I see it all, the wreckage and damage. It is a desolate place. It does not look much different now, despite the time that has passed. There are subtle changes, signs of healing, but it will take eons of time for that place to be habitable once more.

From that vantage point, high above the earth, I can see the whole sad tale play itself out from beginning to end. Imagine, I once told a friend, the horror you would feel, the sheer horror and pathos and awfulness that would grip you by your nuts or whatever you've got, watching a loved one, even a dog you loved, if they were drowning in a cold lake, right before your eyes, just out of reach, you just standing there processing the rapidly escalating feelings—concern to alarm to panic to *this-is-not-happening*—and then that look, the look on the face of your dog or mother or son or wife: *save me.* And then the *slipping slipping slipping* beneath the passive, curling lip of a wave.

And you having always to see that look on their face as the last one—not peaceful or happy but terrified and desperate and alone. Watching Louise die was like that, or worse, drawn out over nearly three years' time like some stop-frame horror film.

The treatments, her doctors—my reasoning mind knows that they were heroic, but in trying to kill the cancer they nearly killed Louise a few times. Cancer is lethal and hard and they go after it hard: with poisons and gasses, knives, lasers, other weapons. In a hundred years it will seem barbaric—hell, it seems barbaric right now. First they cut you up and dig, looking for it that way, looking for all the familiar hiding spots, checking for damage. Then they hook you up, actually build a port right into a mainline artery in your body like a loading dock, and just start blasting poisonous, lethal shit into your body, hoping something works.

They chase that little bug all over you and sometimes they kill it, sometimes they don't. I honestly believe that even the doctors do not know why. Only the cancer knows: sometimes it dies or gives up. Sometimes it just keeps going. It's indiscriminate, has no soul: it takes whom it wants, the young especially. If anything it *prefers* young flesh, devours it like spring lamb.

Cancer is a puzzling, ironic sickness and I was—and remain still—completely baffled by what happened to Louise. I reached no conclusions. I'm speaking of things outside the whole issue of Fate, the problem of God and fairness and why and all that—don't even get me started on that. I'm saying just the whole *medical* thing is so indiscriminate and strange. Admittedly I'm ignorant of much of it, even now: how the disease works, how it takes your body over and starts literally *possessing* your body, replacing all your perfectly good, orderly, working cells with all of its greedy, fucked-up, worthless, lazy little bastard cells. The way it chews on you.

I stuck my head in the sand on that one, mostly due to cowardice. Some people would want the facts: start gathering the virtual mountain of information as though at the peak there were some point that might make a difference. People sent me books, articles, pamphlets. I poked into a couple of things myself, against my guts, because it seemed like the thing to do. But quickly I learned to *hate* the information. It raises more questions than it answers, really, and if you find something that sounds encouraging you will almost certainly find something that completely contradicts it. Unless you're a doctor, or a scientist, here is what you need to know about cancer: ask around, sure, find the best doctor, the best hospital— someone who can make it go away—then pray, sweat it out, hope like hell or whatever you normally would do.

The cure is not in a book, if it is anywhere at all. The books have statistics—frightening statistics that can haunt your quiet hours. I would read something in a pamphlet: *Recent tests have shown that 65% of breast cancer patients who used (such and such chemotherapy) were still alive after five years*...and on and on.

I would get a piece of information like that and it would just work on me for weeks, depriving me of what little sleep I was getting at the time. Was I supposed to be encouraged after reading that? When you are desperately searching for rock-solid hope, you cannot take heart in numbers or statistics. *Five years* they're saying—you might have five good years if you're lucky, if things break right for you. And after a time I did not want to hear anymore about "staying positive" or how "a good attitude can make all the difference" in light of all this cheerful news. I didn't want any glass-half-full bullshit either, not when we were talking about my wife, my daughter's mother.

What I wanted was nothing less than divine intervention, a miracle. I wanted it to settle over her gently, while she slept, like the shadow of a dragonfly. I saw the glass half-full alright, but I was wondering what happened to the other half.

Early on, Louise's doctor told us to forget those figures anyway. Her chance was either one hundred percent or zero, and we had to work for the one while preparing ourselves for the other. Thinking too much can only paralyze you. I knew I was better off cooking dinner, staying on top of the bills, or getting up at night to see about the baby—staying as strong and calm as I could, fanning the flames on our lives—than trying to become the world's cancer expert in a few months. Everything I read about the disease frightened me anyway, so I tried to avoid it. Just reading about it seemed to give it more power, and anyhow I am simple-minded: too much information can overload my circuits and render me useless. I felt I could be more of a help by sticking to the things I could control. *Just keep between the lines, Einstein. Stay steady.* For Louise, I had to be the one thing that didn't change.

So I fly over this wasteland of memory and each time there are new places to discover, uncharted places, places that even my mind cannot abide and is attempting to hide in some remote unreachable outpost to spare me the trouble of remembering…

I do not want to remember, for instance, how it took so long, way past the time when it was obvious, for me to let her know that I knew she was going to die. I was afraid that when I gave up then she, too, would give up, and that perhaps she didn't want to, and I didn't want to see that look on her face, the one I eventually saw, when she gave in. I didn't want to see it and she didn't want to give it to me. We held out for each other, knowing we were only going to make it worse when the time came for it.

When she finally did acknowledge it she was sitting in bed, *another fucking hospital bed* (see how the bitterness remains), and it was worse than you can think, or even remember, the disappointment on her face, the fear, the worst goodbye, the goodbye of goodbye of goodbyes. Her voice was incredulous, almost pleading with me, as though she thought that perhaps I still had a little hope left, and that if I was kind, and if she asked in a nice way, I might share a little of it with her. Just a little hope for one more day. She had become a junkie for hope.

"I don't want to *die*," she said, as though the thought had finally just occurred to her, and in a way—in all of it's finality and awfulness—it probably had.

And me just looking at her, nothing to say, my acknowl-
edgement coming that way, with just a look, inside madly
searching for that small amount of hope to lend her, but
finding nothing. And I'm glad I could not see my face at that
moment—the face of *complicity* almost in its utter
inadequacy, a face to be burned and buried and forgotten—
because seeing hers was too much. I held her tight, pulled
her so firmly close, as though I could pull her right inside of
me where it was safe. I was literally trying to hold onto her,
trying to get hold of some firm *piece* of her. But she was
delicate, and changing beneath her skin. She was turning
into a butterfly.

I am not going to be over this—not ever—I see that now.
It's too big. Certain experiences we are meant to take with
us. I don't see myself as some great tragic figure—not at all.
Plenty of people have suffered this way. Plenty have had it
much worse. Eventually it gets to everyone I'm sure. Maybe
some people don't get it until their last dying minute, but
they get it, finally, the feeling of having had something and
then lost it, however fine or dear to them that it was. A
feeling of being cheated. Or tricked.

I allow myself some selfishness in my grief. I declare a
personal exemption from all infidelity of thought or deed,
rebel against nature as I please. Certain things are
supposedly beyond question, but I'll question them, even
though there are no answers. You will hear answers, or
attempts at the answers, but really they are only
approximations, or explanations, or *theories*. The big joke is
that we are intelligent enough to question things, but are
somehow incapable of grasping the answers. We are garden
slugs with the longings of birds.

To console me, people say things: "She will always live on in our hearts and memories." They are kind words, well intended, and after a while they mean nothing. Memory is a pale approximation and the heart breaks. The past is gone. I want her *here*. Now. With me. The past is even more unlikely than the future—it has already happened once.

Or here's another one: "Try to enjoy what you still have." Well, what choice is there about it? That's what I'm trying for. But the present is overrated too: it is a battlefield strewn with the dead and fresh enemy over the hill.

5

Do you know what is happening outside my window right now? Snow deeper than anything I've seen. It just piles up: snows every day. The whole world lit up even at night, the sky whipped up with snow and the earth snow-laden, deeply drifting, and up there in the mist the snow and sky reflect one another, glowing yellow and orange in the deep pillows of a January sky. Perfect. I asked Louise for this snow. Does she hear me? Does she have such power? I do hear her, feel her. She's here. She would be: she is crafty and always was. She makes herself known to me, almost more clearly now. She is just a reassuring voice, is all. *Sweetie* she calls me. "Mommy's an angel now," I told my daughter, and strangely I believed it.

Meanwhile, the roof of my house is encased in ice! Big anvils of ice hanging from the eaves because the attic is not properly ventilated. I've got to get up there tomorrow: me and my shaky ladder and a hammer and a steep roof thick with ice. I'm about to win the merit badge for Intelligence. See me up there…ah, what a mess. All these little jobs—I need a hired hand. I have not the time nor talent nor inclination to do these jobs. Somebody else do them. There's no division of labor around here anymore—I've got to do it or it won't get done—and it is not my exact fantasy to appear on *This Old House* with Bob Vila. I'm a dreamer at heart. I look out the window and dangle my thoughts from the nearest tree. Loafing is an underrated occupation. I'm tired of all this *can do!* nonsense. I've got more important work to do: taking care of my daughter, taking care of my mind. Now there is some work. I just need some help. I need a *wife*. Trouble is, I want the old one.

January twelfth. It's a date that sticks with me. My old childhood buddy Tom was born on this day. Haven't seen him in years and yet I remember that. He was rare. Came from another big Irish family in the neighborhood. They could all sing. Songs always belting from out of their house. The house rocking and the shutters knocking with their strong, beautiful voices—a duet, sometimes. The open windows breathing song. Like an earthquake when the old man got it going: *Oh Danny boy, the pipes, the pipes they're calling...* I do swear: on a summer's evening, out pedaling your bike low under the big moon, you could hear them singing halfway down the street.

Also I broke it off with Louise once, on this date, several years ago. We had been together about a year at that time. That first aromatic wave of love—that hypnotic time when lovers literally carry the taste of one another in their mouths—had gently passed as it always does, and we had now entered that much more dangerous stage of love when an actual relationship is either forged or lost.

I was having a hard time with this transition, couldn't quite make the leap that was necessary. I was pretty raw, and timid. It was all new to me—Louise was my first serious girlfriend. I backed in and kept the escape hatch wide open. I kept her an arm's length away from me. Frankly, I was a cruel jackass and teased her with my affections: here they are and gone, detached yet living off it somehow, like a parasite. This frustrated Louise. Things built up and she never let things build up for long. Probably, she went a little "over the top" though, as my sweetheart would have put it. She came home to her apartment late from a holiday party and I was there waiting for her—cowering under a blanket, literally—when her "hurricane" (as she later called it) swept down.

She was worked up into some lather about something and very tight as she half-stumbled, half-crashed through the door and began to dismantle her apartment. I remember loud music, huge pieces of furniture smashing to the floor, things being thrown and shattered upon the walls. It was beautiful and frightening: her anger. It was the hook, however painful. I never recovered from that. The hook—I hated it for awhile—but I grew to accept it. I loved it even. Anyway I was a fish and she hooked me that night and of course, like a fish on the hook, I ran. First I ran.

I pondered my escape, and a few weeks later—on the twelfth of January—I broke it off. She didn't see it coming and that was her mistake, really, truthfully. Something needed to happen: me impassive, dumb, like stone—Louise all wild inside, torrents, beautiful, dark and dangerous. Me having cut myself off and her needing passage. It couldn't work. I was cold: it still gives me a chill. Cold the way I said it—*It's over*—and she was frozen with the shock of it, ran to the toilet and threw up, crying *"Really!? Really?"* Me on my knees beside her, reaching for her. She sobbed and held me and it surprised me. I knew immediately that I had made a mistake, but it seemed too late somehow. I cried too, and held her. She felt like a small bird, wounded. Soft in her brown sweater, sobbing and now lonely, heart and breast wounded and pressing up against me. The very birth of a bad memory. That second I started wanting to get rid of it. I've had it since.

It's still snowing.

In the weeks and months that followed we saw each other often. We worked for the same company, and though we tried to avoid one another there were inevitable collisions in the halls or out on the street. It was a torment to me to see her so unhappy, and to know that I was the cause—the surest sign that I still loved her. As the weeks passed her mood seemed to change from sorrow, to anger, to defiance. Then one day even that was gone, and she smiled at me. It had been about two months. We talked briefly. She asked about my friends and I asked about hers. Later that afternoon we collided again before a bank of elevators, both of us on the way home. She walked over and stood before one of the elevators and said: "I think this one." I pointed to another and said "There," and as I did so the light above my elevator blinked red, the bell rang, and we both laughed.

"Have you seen *The Unbearable Lightness of Being?*" I asked her. She had.

"Would you like to see it again?"

She mocked me. "With *you?*"

"Yeah. I'm asking you out on a date."

"Alright."

So we went out. It was a pretty sexy movie. I hadn't planned it that way. We shared a popcorn. I reached for her hand. She didn't pull it away. Before long we were kissing in the movie theater, like kids. We never parted after that, though it was six more years before I asked her to marry me. I do take my time.

This is a box we're in. We are meant to bang our heads up against it. This can be the only explanation. The rules are the same for everyone. All I'm saying is I don't have to like it. I don't have to accept it. I might just keep banging my head until *I'm* dead. Anger flows through me like lava these days. It feels good, actually. I thought I was angry before, but it was so unfocused. Now I am churning deep, raising up some kind of primordial outrage—the sediment of man's ancient howl against the world. I am boiling, boiling.

The knuckles on my right hand, round and red and swollen like a fighter's, bear this out. I punch things—the walls, doors, cabinets, refrigerators. It hurts for a few days, begins to heal, and I start banging it again. Usually it is Robin who sets me off, though she is not the source. I try not to let her see my more volcanic eruptions. It is an overreaction for me to start punching a wall simply because she throws her food on the floor in anger or won't go to sleep at bedtime, and yet that is what it comes to sometimes. As quickly as it comes on, it goes again. I tell her I'm sorry, that it's not her fault. I'm loaded up with dynamite for other reasons. She merely lights the fuse and the whole thing blows right down to the basement. It frightens even me. I'm trying to pull it all in. I'm getting better, slowly.

But I do have some fits—conniption fits that could rip paint from the walls in hell or heaven. I can feel them coming on, the big ones. Tremors start tingling in my very toes and I literally bolt for the garage, close the door and *Funderburk motherscratcher! Fishhead scrapity-scrap-scrapper! Miserable piss-blaster factor! Fichas! Fichas! Fichas!* Slobber on my face, snot. Hair all wild, jumping and ranting like a devil. And it helps, too. Not something you really want anyone to see, but the perfect, beautiful, right thing to do at that moment.

I don't know what I'm raging at, or why. Nor do I have a lack of faith. I do have faith—in what exactly I don't know, but it is there. Everything will come clean. We will all have our peace. But in the meantime, why bow down to it? Why take your beating with pious resignation? If the peace comes with the answers then I will wait for the answers: and rail and spit and chew until they come. Or until I get tired—which will happen, is already happening, I suspect. In the meantime though there is all this fuel: all this piss and nothing to do with it but feel the iron, howl like a raging dog—interpret. Then, maybe later, when I'm tired and spent and all the piss is gone, I can still my mind to reflect the moon.

I go back and forth like this—peace and rage. It's the storminess of it, I know. The storm will end and something will come after. I sometimes think I prepared my whole life to go through all of this with Louise, or that I brought it on by the sheer arrogance of my immortal youth. I've invented two or three dozen new forms of guilt. Did I invite it? Maybe we both invited it.

I'm tired of this existential warfare. One moment I'm talking tough, and the next I'm begging for miracles. Back and forth upon the stormy seas. Should I be prideful and defiant or meek and subservient? Is the question *to whom* do we bow down or is it *whether* to bow down? I'll do it. I just want to know. Whatever I can do to prevent any more bad things from happening.

It is dangerous to keep asking these questions, I know. You'll be driven mad or taken. You get by on asking the safe questions, take what is worth salvaging and leave the rest of that mess behind. Eventually get the focus off yourself entirely: that's a landmark right there. Keep your pain until you're sick of yourself and all your questions, and then just drop everything. It's not worth carrying it all around.

Then what to do? The greatest minds across time and the span of the world have talked about compassion: simply love your brothers and sisters. But I've done that. I loved Louise and it got me here. And here is where I am.

T he thing is this: I'm not sure I have an identity anymore, since she died. It's something I've always struggled with anyway—finding yourself, the old story. But when we met and became friends, then fell in love, became husband and wife, it settled me down, slowly at first and then more completely. It felt good—being loved, depended on, literally like finding your partner or your soul mate. We got a puppy, bought a house, got married, had a baby. Just the right speed for me, not feeling rushed or uncertain (not much), but taking it one breath at a time or close, building something.

Taking slow, certain steps—slow because we both, in the years before we met, had had that flightiness, had gone out into the world looking for something, ourselves, whatever. Eventually you just get tired of yourself and all your longings, realize you can neither escape yourself nor find yourself—that trying to find yourself is, as the guy said, the foolishness at the center of all foolishness: so you may as well just be.

For a long time Louise and I were just making our way, even helping one another, through this painful process of settling down with our lives: pulling each other through it, waiting, falling behind—hating, sometimes. We were both born under Scorpio, if that means anything (we laughed about it). Both of us intense, though my intensity went inward and hers projected out. Both of us black and white and high and low, all clashing, but loving each other because of it, in spite of it—both probably, everything.

You give yourself over to someone slowly, trust finally being the last thing, the jewel you've been searching for all along. Trust is the brick—that cornerstone—upon which you can build everything. That is what we found, and that is what we lost: without Louise our house is teetering now, rickety and unsure and held up by what? I don't know—air, and the way our daughter mingles with it, probably.

It is twenty-six months now since Louise slipped off into the ether. Twenty-six months I've had my foot in the gap where that brick was, to keep this house from tumbling down on Robin's head. I haven't worried so much about my own head, because I've been dead too. I've been following her.

6

I've signed Robin up for lessons at a nearby art school. Yesterday was her first class. She painted a picture of Louise holding a balloon, with long brown hair cascading all the way to the ground. Raindrops fell from cotton-ball clouds in the sky. In the middle were two giant flowers, made from paper cupcake baskets and decorated with colorful sprinkles. There were dried beans scattered upon the ground for the birds to eat. Almost all of Robin's pictures are of her mother. "This is my Mommy in heaven, swinging on a golden swing," she'll say. She draws pictures of Louise in the sunshine, among flowers, or simply holding up a hand and waving at us. Once, she worked intently and quickly on a picture of Louise beneath a rainbow. "Here, Daddy," she said matter-of-factly, pushing the paper across the table in my direction. "It's a picture of your wife."

I have no idea if she'll aspire to be an artist. She can do whatever makes her happy, as far as I'm concerned. She can be an accountant for the IRS if she is passionate about it. But I think her lifelong journey through grief and longing for her mother will be made easier if she can find some way to express herself. This loss does not have to be the central reality of her life, but I know that it will always be right there, like her shadow. It is part of her. She will have to pay heed. I know by my own experience that when some trouble or sorrow settles over you, the best thing to do is to move with it, give it some motion and then let it go. We can free ourselves that way. So Robin will have all the art lessons and music lessons and ballet classes that she can ever ask for.

I can guide her, though I am not much of a teacher. I will be present, always, and can add a trick or two, get her to classes, and encourage her. And perhaps I can be an example to her that grief can be lessened or even tamed through some creative act—that she can recycle her pain by creating something beautiful and unique, take her sorrow and pour it into her pictures or a musical instrument. She has a lovely, resonant voice—she can sing all her longing and loss away eventually, should she choose. She can swallow this experience like a dusty stone, filter it through herself, polish it and throw it back out upon the world—see that it is transformed now, and shining back at her.

A mid-winter thaw. The ice on the roof is slowly melting, though the house has sprung a leak and water is seeping down the wall in two places. Nothing too alarming, and I can't do anything about it now, so I got out for a run today, bundled up in sweats, knit cap and gloves and trudged off with heavy strides through the neighborhood. The sidewalks were slushy and chopped up with ice, banked high—up to five feet—with all the snow that had been cleared, so I kept to the middle of the streets. It was quiet in the half-light of middle morning, the bungalows stiff in the cold, wisps of white smoke filtering up from the chimneys. The houses looked like soldiers in repose, smoking. I pounded it out, a couple miles. Trying to stoke the fire, shake the blues, and it worked, broke up the ice in my soul a little bit. It's easy to get bogged down in this mess. Keep moving—everything, body and mind. You can't sit still. You'll freeze or rot.

I see how I've been fighting depression. It's been a war of attrition ever since Louise became ill years back. You get knocked down and you get back up. This is not a game I relish. Truthfully, I've always been a bit of a quitter. Or, if that's too harsh, I'm at least accustomed to taking the path of least resistance. This is not necessarily the greatest character trait, certainly not the most prized by my many employers over the years. But I've always suspected that I was preparing myself for an entirely different fight than the daily grind for financial security, a pursuit which, though certainly noble when the means are noble, is not a thing I really excel at or take pleasure in.

It occurs that in Louise's illness and death, and in the aftermath—the grief, the loneliness, the difficulties in raising a child alone—I am presented now with a challenge that is really right up my alley. It is elemental, operatic almost, seems to *matter*. It does seem as though I've hand-picked this fight, absurd as that may seem. And now that I've gotten it, I am constantly tempted to quit, to run. It's true: I've wanted to give in on several occasions—could still give in. I respect my opponent, you see: it is there every day, relentless, like an odor or some giant bug. I am not ashamed of this cowardice, only wary. There is something in all of us that wants to quit, to cave, dissemble, dry up and let the wind carry us off into the sweet promise of oblivion. Is it death or nothingness that whispers in our other ear? Are they the same?

I sometimes thought, even before she fell ill, that Louise had a bit of a death wish—only because I've recognized it in myself and I knew her so well—we were similar in that way. Not to suggest that she chose her fate—nobody would choose such a torment. And especially when she became a mother, she fought for her life and her child like a wild animal until there was nothing left.

But there is within us all a deep, deep remembrance of that purity we were born out of, and a secret yearning to return. As Wordsworth wrote: "trailing clouds of glory do we come/ from God, who is our home." Louise felt that tie back to innocence, saw that cloud of glory trailing back into the supernal blue. She was so reverent of it that at times the mortal world seemed absurd to her. Hers was a courageous, but dangerous, tack to play. If life is to be lived on the line then she wished always to float above that line, where the air was lighter, with laughter and love and the ideal.

She was impatient with the details of everyday living— with repetitive toil, pollution and what to do with it, the bills, the mundane (like a roof leaking and paint peeling from the walls). She could be intolerant and would lash out—sometimes at the expense of whoever was near. I certainly caught my share. She genuinely resented it when some unfortunate occurrence drew her unwillingly into the messiness, when the waking nightmare that life can be drew her out of her waking dream, her poetry, her admiration for wildness and beauty. She dared to be a little bit above it all, which some people didn't appreciate or couldn't understand. But for most her charm was seductive, her defiance inspiring, her wit so sharp it could be dangerous—she made me laugh like few people could. She was beautiful. All of us who loved her—myself especially—we were willing to overlook her haughtiness because she had that sparkle, like it was all a performance, and the joke was on you if you took it too seriously. Louise was that rare creature who could infuriate you and regain your adoration in the same instant.

After she died, I wanted to die too—so I could be with her. It occurred to me once, in the first weeks after her death, when I was going through all of her things. I could still smell her as I sorted and folded her clothes—so sensual and immediate was that fading scent of her skin on the deepening folds of cotton, wool, and linen, so freshly present she seemed among the golds and blues of her widowed dresses and orphaned shoes that I swore she might return at any moment as though she had merely stepped out for a gallon of milk.

I had this thought: *I could follow her.*

But if that rogue idea blew in the window with the hollow December gale it blew out just as quickly, to be replaced by immediate thoughts of my daughter, which rose up and around me as though from the basement furnace, circled our bedroom with graceful authority, settled, and warmed me. And still that chilling whisper of death had held, if only for an instant, its own fleeting, intoxicating power. When one so dear has passed into it, death can seem an attractive place. There was a very small, precise moment of choosing, and there was an urgency. The separation was so real and shocking, so final, that I just wanted to go after her, not let her get away. I wanted to find her again. Hadn't I found her once? But she was off and flying and to who knows where. If I was going to go after her, I would have to move. I would have to get on with it, and of course I couldn't.

Your fear is that you're never going to get to see them again, talk to them, hear them laugh. If that was the case—if we are set up to love someone so dearly, only to have them taken and held from us forever—then there really wouldn't be any point to anything, would there? The manufacturer of such a cruel deception would not be worthy of any name, much less God. No, I fully expect—is demand too strong a word?—that I will someday get all of that back, get her back. I'm willing to go along with it all: the long, uncertain future filled with regret for a thing cut short, the real prospect, as a young man, still very young, that my better days and dreams have been aborted, and just in general this life and the rules that nobody seems to understand, if I can have the faith that I will get to talk with Louise again about everything, about us and our daughter, about where she was while Robin and I lived our lives without her. Just to know that she was with us, was watching and helping where she could. That she really had not missed any of it.

If God or whoever can grant me that knowledge, that faith, then I will take what's been given us—what's been scrawled as destiny in the stars for Louise, for Robin and me—I'll take all that with a smile and call it square. I forgive Him.

Robin is a great big handful of a good thing. She gets a little heavy at times—and I do complain—but I am conscious of the comfort that she brings, the consolation. She very certainly holds me to the ground. I would have blown away, I think. I would have sold the house, put my things in a garage somewhere, found someone to watch the dog. I would have flown, and that could have been dangerous, the state I was in.

I still get that urge, even now, when the wind blows. My feathers start ruffling and I think I could just fly away, put some distance between myself and the scene of this tragedy. But then I see that it is all in me, all the heaviness of it, and that I bring myself wherever I go: no escape, not while I'm breathing. What I really want to do is put myself on oxygen, disconnect all the other circuits, climb under a blanket in that garage with all my other possessions and then, while nobody is looking, slip off. Just finally, for a little while, get out from under all this weight.

But there is something that happens when your child is born: you would think you'd see it coming. It is subtle, imperceptible—you don't realize it happened for a day or two, but it did. Your point of reference changed—shifted, really—from yourself to your child. Now she is the center of the universe and you are simply her caretaker, protecting all corners and aspects of her life, a watchdog, supplier of love and food and shelter, lucky enough perhaps to grab a moment or two for yourself when she's asleep. I have become adept, probably to my great disadvantage, at asking questions that make an absurdity of many things, but this is something I can take seriously. Robin. There is a thing worth fighting for. What I said about being a quitter— I could never quit on her.

I look after myself, recognize my own needs. A happy daddy is a good daddy, I tell her. But as sorry as I can feel for myself, there is nothing more unfair than this little girl being deprived of Louise—both as her mother and as the person she was. That's a big hole Louise left when she departed. I do my best, but I can't possibly fill it all. I have huge inadequacies that Robin has already learned to deftly illuminate. I sometimes forget that Robin has to put up with me as well—my black moods and tantrums, my silences. She sets me straight. "Daddy," she said to me the other day, "try not to be such a grump."

I guess my attitude does fall short at times. I always felt I could be a good father—and I think I have been—but this is not mere fatherhood. This is something more. This is a journey now, a mission, and I'm setting off injured and alone. I have to work harder just to keep up. I wasn't overjoyed to lose my wife, to watch her die from cancer. But then in the grip of such heartbreak, when my nerves were wrecked and my confidence gone, to be handed the most difficult and important task of my life—the raising of our toddler daughter alone—that is the stone center of irony. That will get you up early and feeling mean.

But this is what I'm faced with. I'm bound to the task. Any injustices about it can be addressed later. If there is someone behind all this—some creator, or God, whoever— and I ever get the opportunity, I'm going to have to ask: *What the fuck for?*

That kind of anger may indeed be pointless and even blasphemy, but it is well-founded and provides at least a momentary sense of accomplishment. Don't underestimate anger. I may be shooting off into the dark but at least I'm fighting. Anger gets a bad rap in general. Hell yes I'm angry. I feel entitled. It makes me furious to see people knocking my favorite emotion. What happened to Louise and me, to Robin—all of us—that was some kind of celestial rail-job. We lost so much of value—something was *taken* from us. Aside from losing Louise, we lost the roles she would play in our lives: Robin lost her mother, and I lost my wife. We could have used the help.

With just the two of us in the house, it is tough going at times. We both have our moments. Robin cries for her mother, more and more now, mostly when she and I are fighting and she is looking for some comfort. Yes, I *do* holler at my child from time to time. I don't know about other parents. I used to imagine myself a very laid-back guy, seldom had a problem with anyone. But then I met Louise and she had a way of pushing buttons I never knew existed. And now there is Robin. I think the more you love someone, and the more they depend on you, the farther they know they can push you. A child can get you talking to yourself.

So it is not the high point of my day when, at the crux of one of our little battles, Robin turns on the tears and begins wailing for her mommy. This is an insightful tactic she employs, one that turns all my fury shamefully back upon itself. There is just nothing to do with that kind of frustration, no place for it to go. So it comes back. This endless recycling of my own vitriol cannot be healthy. It is a powerful brew, cycling back and through, back and through, growing darker and more acrid, a literal tea of bitterness and pent-up rage, until finally I calm myself as I know I must do, grit my teeth, and swallow it.

When Robin feels I am persecuting her and calls for her mother, I could tell her that her mother would be far tougher on her than I am—which is true—but that would not serve anything. So I don't. I let it disarm me, and more times than not the conflict is over. My empathy for her overcomes my fury. It is such a natural instinct for a child to call for her mother—she calls for her even when she isn't there.

At times I forget, and I think of Robin as having no mother, but she did indeed have her mother for her first two years. She did at least have that, and for many, many days—hundreds of days that were very intense and real. Days that they will always have and that nobody could ever steal from them.

After Robin was born Louise and the baby stayed in the hospital for more than a week. Louise had been through two surgeries and childbirth in the span of a month and the doctors wanted her to get plenty of rest. I brought them home on a Sunday afternoon and we had a little celebration. The house was warm in the early spring and there were flowers and cards from many people. It was just the three of us, our little family, the house bright and warm, a chicken roasting in the oven.

Robin slept but Louise held her for a while anyway and she looked sure of herself and confident, not at all afraid. Finally she placed the baby in her new bassinet for the first time and we sat for a while and just looked at each other. Music was playing and I heard Allison Krauss singing *Baby, now that I've found you I can't let you go* and suddenly Louise was crying softly. I still have a hard time when I hear that song.

Louise cared for Robin almost every day from that time forth, even at times when she was desperately ill. She fed her and bathed her, changed her diapers, read bedtime stories and took turns with me—she insisted—getting up with Robin when she cried in the night. It must have been hard—she was determined—but she knew she had some work to do, knew she had to get herself across to Robin somehow, in case she didn't get much time.

It worked, whatever she did. Some sort of Star Trek mind-melding went on between those two. In watching Robin, I feel as though I'm watching Louise as a child, growing up before me. Often Robin flashes a twinkle, or a glance, that is so like Louise I swear it really is her, that perhaps behind those fierce blue eyes there is a tiny window, and seated behind this window is Louise, working the controls. And I imagine that that twinkle or glance—that knowing, mirthful little spark of mischief—is meant for me, is her way of telling me that she's okay, that she's still with us.

They tease me in this way, this mother and daughter. They gang up on me and have their fun. And had Louise lived, they would have clashed and loved each other madly. It occurs that if there was some grand design to Louise dying, it may in part have been to save me from the lovely, lethal sorcery of these two together. They would have had me stupefied, struck dumb with pleasure and confusion, supping gruel from a bowl like a patient, a benign king in my own house realizing I didn't know anything.

7

The deepest night does not scare me anymore. Anyone knows the lonely terror that visits in the small hours. Lying awake in bed, sirens in the distant blackness hinting of some urgent menace. Napoleon said that the rarest courage was three-in-the-morning courage, but the night is post-apocalyptic for me now. I roam easily through the house in darkness until I find it—The Weather Channel.

How I've come to love it, depend on it. When Louise was sick, I was up every night at two or three o'clock for a few hours. I would prowl and growl in the darkness until I made it to the television and then *poof*—blue light, clouds. All sentiment gone. The cold objectivity of tracking the weather, and yet the futility, too. Snow and rain—the mystery behind it. They can tell us what is happening, but they can't tell us why. That's the beauty of it. Showers in the Northwest, storms in the Texas Panhandle, cut to some poor guy—I love this guy, I want his job—standing on the coast of North Carolina while a hurricane throws coconuts at him. Behind him the churning surf pawing at the shore, indifferent.

Weather, and the gods at play. Something so wild, so superior to us, so contemptuous almost in the way it finds us irrelevant, that we can only try to track it. Louise was like a raisin in our bed near the end, a waif, slight and delicate and curled upon herself and breathing thin. I would curl up around her, envelope her, hold her until I couldn't stand it. And then I was awake—very awake. I'd get up and wander downstairs, pull the blankets up around the baby's shoulders, and then take my seat. Click. Great big map of America, rain in green. Floods in South Dakota. Look at that car spinning down through the swollen river and…whoa…that water is *rough*. There goes the bridge! Big swirl of clouds out over the Pacific. And now your local forecast with a lovely saxophone. The wind and the rain and everything washing away. There must be legions of fans like me. All of us restless in the night, midnight travelers seemingly alone with our troubles until we tune in, watch the hurricane take hungry aim at the rickety shanties of Port-au-Prince.

Just television in general. How it saved us both with its illusion of the utter ordinary. Louise with her soaps and sitcoms, whiling away the endless hours in hospital rooms. And me with my weather, my sports. A very safe, private, yet somehow strangely communal experience. People out there all over the country, all across the world, sharing it with you. How connected you feel without having to risk anything. It's nice. There is no denying that television is a drug, but you can't help liking it. You get your human drama filtered through this magic box, without having to feel anything—just watch, engage the world but from a safe distance. That's how God operates.

We stayed at the summer house of a friend for a week, several months before she died—just Louise and me and Robin, the dog too. Louise was getting pretty wispy and thin, not eating, all bones and angles and her clothes not fitting anymore, and the pain was starting to hit. It was a simple little cottage, but beautiful and bright, sitting up on a big dune looking out over Lake Michigan. There were a few other cottages in view, but the place felt very private. They had just started Louise on morphine, which was like a big flashing sign that told me: "Get Ready."

She liked it, the morphine. It came in a little vial, blue liquid, and every several hours I would fix her a "cocktail" by pouring some into a glass of apple juice. And although we both knew exactly what it signified, I thought of the morphine as a salvation, because at that point I just wanted time with her, as many happy times as we could have. That's what the morphine did: made the time happy, at least for a few hours, where without it the time would have been agonizing, and there would have been less of it.

Things started badly. When we got there it was raining hard. We were drenched simply running from the car to the door. Louise was so sick. Robin was restless from the drive. I was trying to look after them both, get them settled into a strange place. We had forgotten a few important items, as was usually the case when we tried to travel with the baby. We huddled, drenched, inside the cottage. The car was still packed. A vacation? It seemed absurd to have even tried. And Louise was going through the morphine pretty quickly. We realized we hadn't brought enough to hold her and the trip might have to be cut short anyway.

We had bottomed out again—everyone overextended and tired and lacking confidence in one another. Louise and I argued, and we talked about going home. Here was another one of those moments (there had been a few) when it caught up with me. I wanted someone to step in and save me, release me from my contract. I was tired, was all. But I had learned something about endurance, that what you do in such a situation is simply step back, do nothing—*say* nothing, if you can hold your tongue—don't give the moment anymore fuel, and the moment passes and dies like all the other moments.

I unpacked the car. The sea was beautiful—it is a sea, really—and we called the doctor back home and arranged for a pickup of morphine at a pharmacy in a nearby town. We toured the rooms of the cottage. The bedroom window looked out over the water. Louise took a cocktail, opened all the windows, went to bed and listened to the surf, her mind doing what I can't imagine, the colors from the drug swirling among her now familiar terrors, but with the sea calling, blue and deep and far, from some other place. The wind flapped the curtains through the window. She swooned and smiled in the sheets, and so we stayed.

There was something out there, way out in the deep where the sky met the sea—or on the bottom, among the cold wrecks—that was calling her, no question. She was distracted. I started to pay attention, too, trying to understand, just watching the sky and the water, the way it was always different, the way it was always the same. I took Robin down the little path through the bluff to the beach for a while. When we came up later I saw where Louise had a big white blanket laid out on the wood slats of the deck behind the waving grasses. Brightly sunny. Her skinny little body all wrapped up in that white blanket, head and feet underneath it, so slight you almost wouldn't notice a person under there, the blanket rippling in the wind like a kite, as though the whole jangle of rags and flesh and bones might just hover there for a moment, flutter, and blow away. And Louise under there, barely hanging on, curled up and listening to the roar of the surf in her morphine dream.

After a couple of days of resting like this, she began to feel better, and we could get out for a few hours after one of her cocktails. We tried to have a normal vacation. We found a little roadside stand and bought fresh bread, cherry pies, vegetables, fruit and honey. We took Robin to a horse farm, set her up on the saddle of a sleepy pony until she got scared, helped her feed apples to the young colts. There were big cats—mousers—running through the barns and stalls and Robin chased after them. All around the asparagus fields rolled wide and green from the roadside into the wooded hills. The air was ripe and heavy, pleasant with the deep, dew-laden smell of hay and the woods and horseshit.

A big storm blew in off the water one morning. I got up early—even Robin was still sleeping—and watched the gray rolling clouds and the water, gray and rolling too, in the early light. Wind and thunder, sheets of rain. I had a cup of coffee and looked out, thinking how perfect the sea is in the way it is always changing, how it keeps moving and doesn't have to stop and feel anything. Doesn't have to stop at all.

8

Robin and I have settled into some fashion of a routine. We are an odd pair. I love my daughter as any father does, but I also genuinely like her. She is pleasant to have around for the most part, enthusiastic and friendly. She is funny, too, and in the best way—without trying to be funny. Louise was like that. Robin has a funny take on just about everything, and she expresses herself well. She's *honest*. She has a thought and she announces it to whomever happens by. I get some interesting looks in the grocery store from complete strangers. "You're going to have your hands full with that one."

If there is no one else, she talks to herself. Talks to herself all the time, makes up long stories for the benefit of nobody. Once I heard her prattling about something and, thinking she was addressing me, asked her to speak up. She became exasperated. "No Daddy," she said, "I was talking to *myself*. Now please don't interrupt me."

But like her father Robin can get ornery as the situation requires. When her foul mood clashes with my short temper and general impatience, we have some nasty blowups. Again, I have no idea what goes on in other houses. We get along wonderfully most of the time, but occasionally we resemble an old married couple with our bickering. There are flashpoints, certain times of the day when we are more likely to have one of our showdowns. These are usually times of transition—from sleeping to waking, from home to school or back again, from daytime to bedtime. Robin gets on a roll doing one thing, and she doesn't like to be derailed from that. And knowing this, I do not look forward to these transitions either. She has to be coddled through them, and that means more work for me. I try to keep an even keel, try to stay one step ahead of her, so that when she lands in a funk I'm already there and waiting with the solution. But it's difficult to keep this up. I can do it for a day or two, or even a whole week if I concentrate, but sooner or later I fall behind and Robin is right there, plowing on ahead and running right over me.

That is how this job—being a parent—can overwhelm you. You're constantly thinking ahead, trying to clear the way, make things smoother. And it never stops. Anybody can be a hero and do it for a while—like those charming, wonderful fathers you see in the movies who take their kids out for a Saturday afternoon of fun, take them to the ballgame, crash around with them in dodge 'em cars at the carnival, spin them through the park in a horse-drawn carriage. That's the fun part, and we always make time for our "adventures," as Robin calls them. But as with anything else the key to being a good father is in the details. It takes real endurance to do all the little mundane tasks—to keep up with the laundry, prepare healthy meals, help her brush her teeth, read one more bedtime story—and to do it day after day, with some modicum of patience and enthusiasm, to keep it up for weeks, months, years.

Mornings are hardest here, as witnessed by the Great Underwear Incident of '99 for example. There are countless other chilling tales of the A.M., most of them less amusing, more mundane, and therefore more deeply repressed in my mind. Just getting the whole machine revved up and organized and pushed out into the world can be hard. We do not have "normal" days here, but a *typical* day finds Robin rising in a mood that is at best tolerant, and at worst most foul. When I have to get to work and Robin to pre-school, we do not always get off to the best start. We are not morning people. I don't enjoy going in to wake her up anymore than she enjoys the intrusion. She does not exactly spring into her day. When she finally gives in to the inevitable need to rise, she more or less flops herself into my arms like a rag doll and I have to carry her to the breakfast table (thinking to myself one of these days this nonsense is going to *stop*).

Of course this morning phobia all comes down to attitude, does it not? And who am I to lecture on this subject? But I can point to the weekends to illustrate my point. If it is Saturday or Sunday, Robin rises on her own as though she were shot out of a cannon, often before seven o'clock in the morning. She then rouses me by coming to the base of the stairs and hollering, at the top of her voice, "Cock-a-doodle-doooooooooooo!" with an artful roll of the tongue upon the last syllable. A fitting opening salvo to a daylong monologue that often cackles happily along, usually with no intended audience, until it finally trails off to a hoarse whisper in her bed at nine o'clock that evening.

But on "school" days Robin will from time to time wake up in a *selective* mood, to put it delicately. Only slightly ahead of her on the outlook curve at this point, I am as eager to please as I am intolerant of any unreasonableness. In short, I want to keep Robin happy, but I'm not about to take any crap. When I wake up, I am already behind schedule. In less than an hour I must feed her breakfast and pack her lunch. I've got to lay out clothes for her and get myself fed. I must shower, dress, and warm up the car. Inevitably, throughout I must continually cajole her to get dressed and ready as she seeks refuge beneath a blanket before the television.

And there is always enough time—barely enough—to accomplish all of this, provided that no problems arise. But there are always problems—tiny adjustments that need to be made in order to keep Robin's fragile mood balanced in its perfect place there beside the peak of ecstasy and above the valley of despair.

For instance, today Robin informed me (after I had already made her breakfast) that she did not want oatmeal, she wanted cereal. And she didn't want the nutritious, healthy cereal that Daddy eats—she wanted the chocolate, Scooby-Doo cereal with marshmallows. And did she want toast? She did, yes, but she wanted it with butter and honey—with the honey to go on first, and *then* the butter. And while she did appreciate the apple slices, she did not think that she could actually eat them—she was suddenly full and did not believe she could eat another bite actually—and so she wished to retire to the living room for a little television. She did *not* wish to get dressed immediately, she informed me, but she would certainly be dressed when it was time to go. Meantime, she was cold. Could I please cover her with that warm blanket from over on that other chair? And could I also bring her a cup of chamomile tea—not too hot—to sip and warm herself by in her viewing?

Let me be quick to point out that this is not how things actually went down.

It would have been, had I been an utterly spineless houseboy with no interest in anything other than complete tranquility. But I am her Father, first and foremost, a rank and title that carries with it a certain regality. Or barring that at the very least it commands a little more respect. In my perfect world I would be the kind of father who rules by a sort of weary but lighthearted *intimidation*, a benevolent dictator seated high above the fray. Picture Mr. Bennet in *Pride and Prejudice*, emerging only occasionally from the sanctuary of his library to put forth his decree and then quietly retreating to his worn, leather-bound book of poems as the house goes into an uproar all around him.

Unfortunately, my role can more accurately be described as that of Robin's "parent"—a far less glorified, more practical, even proletarian title better suited to these enlightened times. I struggle with this new identity. I suspect that I have lost something: my *manhood* perhaps? A man can be a father and a parent at the same time, I suppose, but that does not change the fact that all evidence points to the males having lost considerable ground in the battle of the sexes. The modern father has come to be expected to handle a great deal more of the "parenting," whatever the hell that means. I guess I should at least give lip service to the idea that this is more equitable and fair, but that doesn't mean we have to like it. Wasn't a father once placed upon a pedestal far atop the hill? What are we doing down here with all these diapers and bottles and mess? It is valuable ground we have lost.

We may be better parents now, better fathers even, certainly better husbands in most women's minds which I guess is the ultimate point behind it all really. But in coming down from the mountain of Fatherhood to the wasteland of parenting, we have lost something. I say this only partly in joking. I only need to point to the man we've become, the ideal father and husband, hero of the women's magazines, the talk shows, the television sitcom, even the movies. He's a guy you have seen ten thousand times in the mall or the park or wherever, trailing along behind his stroller-pushing wife, wearing sensible sneakers and lugging the extra-large diaper bag, tapping his watch and whining, "Honey, we really need to be thinking about getting him home for his late morning bottle or the afternoon schedule is going to be all out of whaaaaaaaack…"

I could see where a woman with children would want to have a guy like that around. But I could also see where he's fallen a certain estimation in her eyes. Useful, but a little bit emasculated.

And anyhow in my case the point is moot. I've got to be mother, father, *and* the houseboy who does all the dirty work. And this was dirty work at seven o'clock this morning. Fourteen degrees outside and still darker than a cave on an ordinary Tuesday. Robin was laying down a familiar gauntlet of resistance and it was my job—as her parent—to get down there into all those dirty little details and keep the train moving.

And so began the haggling:

(re: Oatmeal versus cereal) "Yes you can have cereal this morning, *Your Royal Highness* (sarcastic emphasis mine)— right after you've finished the oatmeal I already made for you. And you may not have the Scooby-Doo cereal today. That's for weekends only—which I believe today is not."

(re: Toast and honey) "I will not put the butter on *after* the honey. That is simply a ridiculous request—they get all mixed up together anyhow and if you don't like it you don't have to eat it.

(re: No apples—request to watch television) "You can definitely watch television—just as soon as you've finished eating your apples. I don't spend time making you breakfast because I think it's a big barrel of fun."

(re: Fetching the blanket) "I really cannot see myself covering you with that blanket—you are not a baby anymore, and you are perfectly capable of walking over there and getting it yourself."

(re: Chamomile tea—not too hot) "I will make you a cup of tea, just as soon as I've finished with the four other chores I'm in the middle of. And I'm not going to *serve* it to you—when it is ready I will call you and you can come into the kitchen and get it yourself. Here are your clothes for the day—please do not make me beg you to put them on three minutes before it's time to go…"

We will go back and forth on a few of these points, both of us winning a concession or two. Robin is a dogged negotiator. She keeps coming, in waves. Whatever points she did lose on today, she will raise them again tomorrow. She knows that she has key advantages—principally that she doesn't give a damn if we're late, that I will often concede a dearly held principal in the interest of expediting things. I know this because that poorly suppressed smirk on her face betrays her, tells me she is aware of my weaknesses and will exploit them unmercifully. And these talks are always highly sensitive—at any point, and principally at Her Majesty's discretion, they may completely break down, all civility and dignity tossed aside, and we quickly find ourselves in an ugly incident complete with tears, name-calling, slamming doors, and a tight schedule gone all to hell.

I shudder to think of mornings in our house had Louise lived. Were she to descend from the clouds on Wednesday, we would have an ecstatic Wednesday evening—and an awful Thursday morning. Louise was not a morning person either, to say the least. Like me, she was perfectly happy in the morning, provided she did not have to speak to anyone before ten. I learned to walk the long way around her—learned it the hard way actually. She was like a cat. Get too close and she might suddenly hiss and lash out a long paw and rake your neck for no apparent reason. Nothing personal. Two minutes later she'd be sitting in the window seat taking in the morning light. She'd kiss me on the cheek and say good morning as if nothing ever happened.

We learned to avoid one another before noon on working days. My morning routine became stealthy and efficient—I would rise first, run a quick shower, get dressed, drag a comb through wet hair, and head out the door as Louise stumbled about half-asleep in the kitchen. There was rarely anything of real importance to talk about at that hour. Part of good communication is knowing when to shut the hell up. Our entire affinity worked best on that principle. Louise and I both required plenty of space, and we were smart enough to give it to each other, contemptuous as we both were of those (in our minds) overly needy, verbose, suffocating relationships we had been witness to. Together we were like an atom of helium, two high-flying electrons rotating happily in our orbits about the same nucleus. We knew that if we got too close a cataclysmic explosion was likely. It was a volatile, potentially explosive relationship that would have blown up in the faces of mere amateurs—but one that was beautiful, light and airy when handled by professionals, with great care.

So it would have been interesting to see how we would have worked it out, our mornings with Robin. While Louise and I had learned to walk the long way around one another, there can be no avoiding a child. It's part of the deal. They have a hard time getting through some days, and they need our help, need us to be there while they struggle with it. It can get dirty. We have to let them push us around a little, so they know how far they can take things. And we have to push back sometimes, so they know how it feels. Louise would have brought some dynamite to the party, no doubt. We would have blown the roof off the house, some days. I smile to think of it.

Annie comes to stay on the weekends. Robin likes her, looks forward to Fridays when Annie comes over. It isn't difficult to see why. The house comes more alive. Annie is cheerful. She *talks*. I'm a little weak in these areas. We have a good time. We all go together on our adventures during the day, then in the evenings we cook. We grill in summertime, and in cold weather we make monstrous stews that simmer all day, let the aroma warm the house. But by Monday Annie is gone again, back to her apartment in a nearby town, and Robin and I have our week together. I like it this way. I think Annie is starting to look for something more.

Do I have the dreaded "fear of commitment"? Hell yes. I tell Annie that it is nothing personal, and this is true, but I don't think she's going to buy it much longer. She could have her pick of guys. She could drop me tomorrow. My head has been on the block on more than a few occasions— one of these times the axe might come down. That will be a problem, but I have to be ready for it. I could no easier make any serious commitment now than flowers could start blossoming out there in the snow. Not hell or heaven could budge me right now. In many ways I am a pushover, but in matters of the heart I am resolute: I move for nothing without total conviction.

So Annie waits a while longer. We both do. I have no idea what's going to happen. It's difficult to conduct a new relationship while you're still mourning your wife. I don't think I'm going to win the Nobel Prize for making that discovery. I'm living more deliberately. With each passing day I feel more free, less inclined to do anything, as though I am in the process of unburdening myself of something and that has to come first. I have to allow myself that. It is actually taking place.

For the first time I can remember I have absolutely no expectations for the future. I could get married again and start a new family. I could resolve to be a bachelor, raise my daughter alone, enjoy the sprawling luxury of my solitary bed, call all the shots without static or compromise. This does not seem all that impossible. I have fewer illusions now. I've been married once. I've been backstage, saw the puppet dancing on the string.

I could do it again. There is just no hurry. I'm about as bright as the new moon. It will have to be the right time, the right person, the right place even, all three so obvious the notion will have to bludgeon me over the head a few times before I'll see it. This starting over is so filled with possibilities it can paralyze. Even before the first step you have to choose a direction. I've even thought of moving to another state for a time, or another country. But I suspect that this place—this cradle where all my family and friends still live—will always be home. Flight rarely solves anything. Your troubles only come with you and you leave your solace further behind. As Yeats said, "I must lie down where all the ladders start,/ In the foul rag-and-bone shop of the heart." By not leaving I save myself the embarrassment of the inevitable return with my tail between my legs. Whatever will happen is going to happen here.

And something will happen eventually. Only not soon. I'm slowing it all down. How slow is slow? Slow as a *tree*. Let the world grow me for a change. Slow enough to where the question is, "Do I breathe, or does it breathe me?" That is how slow. All the pressure is off. I'm just living. I've told Annie this many times. Each time the door was wide open and she stayed and I was glad.

Increasingly my friends are women, or at least the friends I actually talk to. This is more alarming than any backhanded attempt to make myself appear "sensitive," if only because it hints at changes in me more radical than I admit to myself. My male friends are spread all over the world, or they are just busy. We talk so seldom. Many of them are doing very well, running their own businesses and making a lot of money. Most are married and have families of their own. As the years pass I see more and more of my married friends settling into the lives our parents lived—the man works and the woman (always with a modicum of regret) stays home and raises the children. They settle into these roles more out of practicality than tradition, because in most cases she is simply better at handling children and he is better at making money. I must admit I envy those guys sometimes. I'd love to be able to walk out the door every morning and go to a job that gave me at least a parcel of satisfaction, then come home to my happy little family every night. Knowing what I had to do and then doing it, never questioning.

I don't know if Louise and I would have ever settled on such an arrangement, but that is almost beside the point.

It's a fantasy. I see happy couples and their small children and it looks nice. I'll see a guy and his wife and I'll think: *That guy has a nice wife.* Just like that, as though I were sizing up his new car. I don't desire his wife or think about stealing her away. I try to put myself in his shoes, understand how happy and content he is to be married to someone he loves, someone he can talk to and share his love of his children with. I'm happy for him. I think how I had that once, how maybe someday I'll have that again.

Maybe someday I can be that superhero breadwinner father who works in an office all day—or better yet, goes out to the barn and creates massive, unfathomable and expensive works of art—while his beautiful wife cleans up all the messes at home. Quiet evenings together on the porch. Weekends free. All of that seems far off. Whatever kind of career I had going is now a joke. It really wasn't ever much to begin with. I was trying to find something that worked for me when all this trouble began. I'm still looking. Maybe I would have found it by now. We'll never know. Mostly I'm a father these days. It takes up almost all of my time. There doesn't seem to be anything else nearly as important.

Soon I'll have to figure something out. I've been floating for a while now, first on the pardon of my employer and now lately on the generosity of my family. But the gravy train is about to reach the station. I joke with my friends that I need to meet a rich woman doctor, so I can sit around all day eating bonbons and watching soap operas on television.

I'm starting to hear the smartass comments, too. "When you roll out of bed this afternoon can you give me a call?" Or, "How are you enjoying your retirement?" Poor misled jackasses. I don't even try to defend myself. Everybody works harder than you, and they want to make sure you know. When somebody tries to make me feel like I'm slacking off, I tell them they can take over for me anytime. One week in my shoes and they'll go running back to their lives before their mothers know they're gone.

At parties, while the men sit around and talk about golf or business, I find myself more frequently drifting toward the kitchen where the women are sitting. I don't even want to think about what that means. It's just true. I'm gathering information, looking for some solidarity. We talk about our kids. This almost always makes me feel better because I learn that other people's children are just as insane as mine. I get some important tips, too, even pass on a few things that can help someone else. One time, before she even knew what she said, a woman friend of mine beckoned me over for some "girl talk." My feelings were hurt for about two seconds—I wanted to beat her with a heavy stick—then I followed.

The traditional roles are all breaking down anyway. At this point in life, and in my situation, what difference does it make? *Be who you are at the time, I tell myself. Be the Daddy and the Mommy too.* Make no mistake, I can sit and drink beer and rip gas and scratch myself with the best of men, but now out of necessity and because I feel like it I reach out toward what are considered the more feminine graces, which are just more useful. I cook and tend to my flowers and vegetables. I listen to opera, and I keep a damn tidy home if I do say so myself. Mighty tidy. In fact by some people's first impression I probably seem as gay as a day in May. Whatever. I'm just trying to make a nice home for my daughter. I'm the Mommy and the Daddy. I am who I need to be at the time. The Mommy can get those whites whiter, and if you've got something to say about that the Daddy can knock your head off with a football from forty paces.

I realize now I'm in the middle of my life. I can see all around me. The past is sizeable enough—plenty has already gone down. The present is the universe, going off in every direction. And the future is like some mysterious fruit, delicious but possibly dangerous. It seems like you should do something here, at this point, this high ground. You should build something, put a flag in the ground. You should remember this place, so you'll know what it was you were building up to, so you'll have something to look back on. This is the middle. It's not a bad spot. The regrets haven't caught up with you and there is still time.

Noon and blue sky, brightly sunny and yet a flurry swirling gently down from some high distant cloud. My little house and a window toward the day. I imagine a fireplace over in that other corner. In lieu of that I have the smell and heat of a warm dog at my feet.

This dog. She's a little nuts. She gives me more than I can handle. In another time she would have been marched down the road, pulled off under a low clearing, and shot. Fortunately for her, I'm still wearing this "S" on my chest for Sucker. I could never do it. Stella Blue takes advantage of my good nature. I shake my head.

She's a pretty girl, an eight-year-old Shepherd-Husky type mutt, compact (fifty-four pounds) and strong—black on top and all white underneath with brushes of burnt sienna. She has Cleopatra eyes. Her ears are like a military instrument, sharp and battle-ready, able to pick up a rumble of thunder as far away as Indiana. She hates thunder, gets all flustered with even a sniff of foul weather. This dog is nervous, hard-wired. She gets the shakes when a storm is coming, or even when she just *imagines* a storm coming. She whines and follows me from room to room throughout the house panting short, shallow breaths like a junkie, constantly underfoot, pressing herself up against me as though I were a security blanket. I would never kick her, but I've wanted to. I've wanted to boot her right back to that farm where we found her. I would march her up there with her bowl, a bag of dog food and her leash and say, "Here! Goddamn dog is nuts!"

I am overloaded already to have to deal with a needy dog. She has to be walked every day or she's just murderously psychotic. It is too much but I do it, along the way muttering to myself through clenched teeth, "There really is something *seriously* wrong with you girl." Most people would have given her up. I can't do it. She's a part of the family. She and I both would bite the man who tried to take her away.

Stella is grieving too. I know that. But she stands there looking at me, so anxious. She sees some imaginary four-foot box around me and wants to stay *inside* of that box at all times. I feel her hot dog breath on my leg. I see her fur flying, dropping everywhere, and I know that I'm going to be sweeping it up. Tumbleweeds of fur rolling into the corners of every room. This dog, all her mess and the way she crowds me—it's like having two more people in the house. I guess I'm a little edgy myself, here in my little house with my daughter and my neurotic mutt and all my goddamn chores. It presses in. We're all crowded in our grief. That is probably the best way, though it can be a little tense. I want to say—and I do say—"Stella darlin', I love you girl but back the fuck *off!*"

But she is a stubborn, willful animal, and I am her master. They talk of how a dog sees its master as a pack leader—imprinting they call it. If that is true then my countenance must be etched onto her brain like a vision of the Madonna. She would gladly follow me into hellfire or worse. I appreciate her loyalty, but if I must have a dog I find myself at times wishing for one of those obliging, dimly lit Labradors.

"Take it easy, dog," I'll mutter in frustration. "You can be a part of the family by just lying down there in the corner." But she keeps on with that look, that pleading dog look, eyes all soulful and searching. "And don't look at me that way. If you're looking at *me* for answers you really are nuts. Think of all those other dogs. Take a moment to enjoy your good fortune. Dogs all over this world that would give their right paws for the life you lead. Kick back and relax. Sleep!"

9

I went to a funeral the other day, for the mother of my sister-in-law. She had been ill, but it came as a shock anyway. She was a sweet lady, very religious in the best sense, in the sense that she had compassion, tried to help people. It was the first funeral I had been to since Louise died, and it brought some of those old feelings back.

I choked up a little. I don't know why I'm surprised when it comes back and hits me again. It got me at this funeral, when the music started, when the family came up with the casket. I was back on that beautiful, sunny December morning more than two years ago, riding to church with my brother and his wife and Robin, heading to the memorial mass for Louise.

Robin had stayed the night before at my brother's house, so that I could have some time alone to work on a poem I was going to read. I went over in the morning in my new suit that I didn't like, still don't like. Robin was playing with her cousins. She didn't know what was happening, didn't even know that Louise had died. As far as she knew Daddy and Robin lived at home and Mommy lived at the hospital. She thought it was a big adventure.

She was still in her sleeper when I got there. I had brought her little red dress, tights, patent leather shoes, red woolen coat. I bit into a bagel—my mouth was dry and I couldn't swallow it. This was going to be hard. I laid Robin down on a bed to get her dressed. I still didn't know what to tell her. "Your mommy's in heaven now," I told her. "She was so sick that her body just stopped working and she died." I looked in her eyes for a moment. She knew I was serious. She just nodded her head and oddly smiled at me. She twirled her fingers in her hair.

"She's very happy in heaven," I said. "She's not sick anymore. Today we're going to a church, and everyone who loved her will be there. We're going to say goodbye." I hadn't rehearsed anything and it came out that way. She didn't seem to get much of it. "But you know what?" I added. "She's still with us! We just can't see her. She'll always be with us. She'll be with you most of all, because she loved you most."

Her look told me that I was scaring her now. I think she thought I was joking. I don't think she understood my words, and my tone of voice probably frightened her. It seemed inadequate, but it would have to do. Something we would have to work on together.

It was time to get going. I didn't want to do this, the whole day. I just wanted it to be over, get past it. I was tired of it all. All these final scenes, all this heed being paid to a singular unspeakable fact, me and my two-year-old daughter in the hot lights.

We rode through the quiet neighborhood to the church, pale autumn sunshine, shadows across the road like fingers from the black branches of the trees. Then Robin did something curious. Looking out the window, in her dreamy state, one foot bobbing on the back of the seat, she suddenly started saying the word "Mama" in a soft, sing-song voice. "Mama…Mama…Mama…" she kept saying, sweetly, hypnotically, like a mantra, over and over again, the others of us in the car struck dumb and looking off in different directions, that little voice the only sound in the world right then.

Louise was right there! I could feel her presence, truly, but for Robin—it was as though she could *see* her, too, as if Louise was just outside the car window, looking in, sending some kind of pure love that only a child can comprehend. And while I remember that now so vividly, and it does give me some comfort, at the time it seemed to lay me open even more. I was raw with emptiness and dread, wondering if this was as bad as it was going to get, or if there was more, if it could possibly get sadder than that.

We pulled up. Big crowd of people outside the church doors already—Louise's mother and brothers, all my family, dozens of friends. Eyes on me. You would never think to imagine this. Not too far back there had been a wedding and all the same faces had been there.

I just wanted to push through that crowd, keep going, put about ten years behind me in the next forty seconds. But we would have to do this. I stood there not knowing what I was supposed to do. My mother grabbed my hand. "They're waiting for you to go up."

Alright let's get it going. So we walked up, Robin and I, holding hands. The church was empty. A place for us right up in the front row. At the front of the aisle, up before the altar, a white pedestal. On top a single framed photograph of my wife's face. I remember snapping the picture. Black and white. She was sitting on my brother's back porch, summertime, pretty in her pearls, my tweed jacket draped over her shoulders in the evening light, a half-smile and a sideways glance, bangs of hair across her forehead, one eyebrow slightly raised: knowing.

Like walking to your execution. We took the front pew, people coming in behind us. That heavy organ sound, lonesome and antique. I kept seeing that photograph. *Can I hold back this crying? Can I do it? Should I, even? I don't want to lose it right here. Don't look at that photograph. Don't look at the people. I want to hide but there's nowhere to go. Please let the priest come out. Please let's start. Now here he comes. Okay, that's better: words.*

The whole power of all those people behind me in the church. *I can't look at them. I've got to read this thing I wrote. Maybe I won't. People will understand. No, for her. All she did, I can do this one thing. Get up there. If you were ever meant to do anything, you have to do this. Okay honey, help me. You'll help me, yes. We'll get through this together. Stand up for her. But I don't want to. But you must! You get up! You walk up there and do this for her right now.*

So I did it. I got through it. My voice broke a few times and I had to stop once, but I did it. I sat down and kissed Robin on the top of her head. My mother grabbed my hand and said "That was fine." *Okay sweetheart, that was for you and I'm glad I did it. All your pain is my pain now. Give it all to me and I'll know what to do with it. Rest, my darling wife. Rest easy.*

Well I don't want the pain anymore either. I've got it pinned to the ground. I just want to make sure she's clear and safe—long gone and free—before I let it up. I'm going to wrestle it into a cage and drag it out into the wilderness, drag it by sled all the way to the top of the tallest wind-rippled glacier in Antarctica, peer down into some narrow, miles-deep crevice, and pitch it over the edge.

I want to think about something else for a change. These emotions have scattered me for too long. I need to get specific, attend to questions that have answers. I envy a scientist and his pure research. The way he can focus in on one thing, find something small and true, publish his paper, add to the heap of human knowledge, go home. Or better yet a guy who can build things—shelters, gardens, giant sculptures that serve no purpose. Small, elemental things that people find useful or comforting, or things that are perfect all to themselves. Things that can be done quietly. How fine it would be to have your place, a few friends around, and tasks at hand. Or just the time for useful tasks. Also plenty of time to do nothing.

I'm going to keep it even simpler from now on. I'm going to try to avoid any collective ambition. I saw a war movie today—*The Thin Red Line*. Men from both sides of the battle thrown into a cauldron that no single man's evil intent (it takes a collective evil) could conjure up by itself. The war serving no point but to show men its face, hope they learn something. I think I know how those soldiers felt when they got to the top of the hill, began to overrun the enemy— when they saw the terror in the eyes of men who until that time had been an abstract evil—their utter disillusionment. The hate they encountered, that they summoned up in themselves, to find that the enemy was just like them.

Keep going along and you'll find how absurd it all can be. That's what they found out, but by then it was too late. They were stuck: orders. And nature was swallowing them up—the jungle literally absorbing them, dragging them back down. Far more intelligent creatures up in the trees, watching, waiting. At the end that coconut in the tidal pool, sprouting up into a tree: hopeful.

Amidst all that futility, everything just keeps trying.

II

Water

10

I know I've got to think about moving on. I'm desperate for some useful work. The job I have is just that—a job, a pretty good one. Doesn't pay a lot but it doesn't ask for my soul the way some people's jobs are now doing. It's a pretty big company, takes care of its people well, has taken care of me. Quite objectively I've been a piece of shit around there for a few years, but they recognize my difficulties and keep me on.

It's been a long haul. Through the cancer treatments and trying to help Louise with the baby—trying to run our household so she could do what she needed to do—and onward through her agonizing slide downward, and her death, and then, after, the grief and raising our daughter alone: my job has seemed far away. I go into the office to rest, mostly. It is the only break I get.

This struggle wears you down. It gets you high and low. There is the big issue, of course—the life and death struggle, which occupies your brain with all the subtlety of a two hundred pound buzzard farting in a small room. And then there are the little daily tragedies that keep hammering away. It's a tag team: they work hand-in-hand. When you're losing hope that the big battle can be won, it makes it that much harder to deal with those little things. And if you're not taking care of those little things, the big issue will certainly be lost. It is a self-defeating spiral of futility that can only be countered by keeping your emotions steady, by not letting them get drawn into it. You have to turn your emotions off, if you can. You have to be cold almost. You can't get caught up in the little victories any more than you can let the disappointments drag you down.

It takes a great deal of energy to clamp down on your emotions like that. You have to literally get on top of them and *sit* on them. I remember catching glimpses of my reflection in a mirror or a shop window and being surprised at the fierce expression on my face, the look of a scout or a prophet on some biblical mission—perhaps I was only going for a loaf of bread—the stitched brow, eyes focused, lower lip curled as though I were staring into the teeth of some great storm and was biting down, riding it out.

And I know the popular wisdom says you are supposed to feel everything. It's unhealthy to hold your feelings inside. You're supposed to let your emotions out, express yourself. I see the wisdom in that now, but if I had followed this line of thinking back then, when the action was really heavy, I would have been sitting in a corner most of the time, crying. That's what I *felt* like doing—crying, or running away or complaining or shooting myself. I would have been useless, or even destructive, expressing all my feelings.

I don't know what I was, but I wasn't useless. I could have been better, could have done more. But I was trying hard, doing some good, and it seemed to work better when I was keeping my feelings down. There is a time for crying, for expressing yourself. That's what I'm doing now. I'm trying to get rid of it. That's the way with your feelings—when you get them, you can only get rid of them. But at the proper time, in a safe place. You don't just drop your trash as you go. Do it at a more convenient time.

But do get rid of them alright. Rid yourself of your feelings and become perfect again. Nothing perfect has any feeling left. Flowers blowing out there in the field feeling nothing—beautiful flowers.

So, when I went to work I had nothing on my mind but recharging my batteries. I wasn't getting any rest at home. I needed to get it somewhere. And as bad as I was having it, I knew Louise was in some other realm. But she kept working hard. I felt small next to her as I saw her fight so hard. If it sounds like we were both fighting it on different fronts—well that's how it was. Heavy combat. It divides you. Together we had a whole line to defend and we were both running around filling holes as we saw them. You don't even have time to stop and talk about how it's going. Looking back on it now, I worry that perhaps I should have been more right *next* to her, that we should have been slugging it out more together than we were. That feeling that you left someone abandoned, uncovered—now there's a pleasant feeling. There is something to ponder for another forty years. That guilt is gnawing away on the electrical wire.

By the time I got to my office in the morning I was already beaten down. We had help during the worst periods, but throughout much of her chemotherapy Louise insisted on caring for Robin when she could, despite the awful nausea and weakness that came and went. A typical morning would find me getting Robin her breakfast while Louise was face-deep in the toilet, throwing up. She would rebound from that and tell me to go ahead and get to work. But some days I couldn't leave her like that. I would call my mother to see if she could come and sit with the baby for a while, so Louise could rest. Or if Louise was feeling better, perhaps it was Robin who was sick with a cold, or being fussy and cross. Sometimes Louise would snap at the baby, to the point where I thought they shouldn't be left alone together. Or some mornings I would find Louise sitting there in her chair, holding the baby in her arms, crying. Rough and desperate already at eight in the morning, all hell breaking loose, and while there was no way I wanted to bail out on a situation like this, I simply had to work. I needed the job. I didn't earn much, but we needed the money. And we really needed the health insurance.

Finally, as happened on many occasions, my mother would arrive to save us all for another day, and I would head out the door and go to work. Driving down the freeway, consumed with guilt at having left, I wanted to turn around, go back home and help in some way. Or hide. My place was obviously at home—my job and what I did there seemed ludicrous in comparison. And anyway, after a morning like that my meager concentration was broken for the day. I'd sit at my desk, have a cup of coffee, make some calls, play around on the computer—tired and sick of everything, the stress beating on me and me beating it back. To my colleagues I was like a ghost, insular in my comings and goings, quiet, that self-perpetuating black silence surrounding me: not wanting to talk to anyone, or wanting to, but not able to bridge it, the distance.

On many of those mornings, I would no sooner sit down than there was a phone call, from home or a hospital or a doctor's office. Some emergency, some minor or major crisis, and could I please come, could I please hurry. And I

would be up and running back to my car, passing people
still on their way in to work, wanting to leap home,
planning my ninety-miles-an-hour path up the expressway:
the urgency. I'm coming. Tears in my eyes if the news was
real bad, swearing, beating the steering wheel with my
hands, flying through heavy traffic.

If that call didn't come I would just sit for a while, enjoy
the luxury of doing absolutely nothing. At noon I'd walk
through the city streets to my health club. I loved my
workouts, cherished the time alone, the sweating, beating it
into the machine—in my mind killing cancer cells, legs
churning, grinding, chasing, scattering them. I pounded on
that machine, escaped by watching sports highlights on
television. And then I would have a quiet stretch, alone in a
bright room, the whole club to myself at that time of day,
sunlight in lines across the wood floor, almost religious the
way I postured and reached.

For lunch I would eat a big sandwich, soup, some
cookies, my head clear and above the clouds now: that
relaxed body buzz from a good workout and a big meal. I'd
work a few hours in the afternoon until there came the itch
to get back home, back into the mess, see where I could take
over. Feeling restored, ready for it. Giving myself a little
pep talk.

You have to get a little bit bigger than this…

Or fighting the urge to feel sorry for myself.

*You can keep it up because she needs you to keep it up. You can
rest later…*

Every day being down so low and having to find the way
back up.

It's so much harder for her. As long as she can, then so can I.

I was guilty about not contributing much at work, but if
I had to choose between home and work—and I did have to

choose, it seemed—the choice was easy. There was some tension with my co-workers. Solitary the way I came and went, outside their workings, outside their group. My work was half-assed and I knew it, admitted it, made sure they knew that I knew, hoping they would understand. Of course they did. They all took on more to cover for me. I tried to show my gratitude, but I don't know if it came across. I was buried under my personal life, so removed from the work, what they all did. There was not much in the way of professional talk. New projects came along, new systems and software. I kept falling farther behind.

Maybe they wanted me to share it with them, so they could better understand, but I became more withdrawn. I did not—*could* not—care about work: all my caring was being used up elsewhere. I just wanted to show up, rest, get paid. I would have been bitter too, to see a guy coming and going like that, not acknowledging anyone, taking his paycheck and splitting at three in the afternoon. But there was only so much of me to go around, and I wasn't going to spend much of it at work, not if I could get away with it. And I could get away with it, apparently. I used them all, in a way. I would do it again.

It's still going on, actually. To this day I am lost at work, a liability. It's getting ridiculous now. I've got to make a move. I've been taking some time off, and I don't know if I can go back there. The whole thing is played—it too much resembles an old cage I've broken from. Louise and I met there. The place holds so many scenes of a past I am trying to forget—connotations of failure all around. I guess that's it: I feel like a failure when I'm at work. Really I feel like a failure at everything—not a complete failure, but enough of one. Enough to make me worry that the problem may not lie solely within the circumstances. Maybe it's me.

When you get so consumed by something, as I have been consumed by this tragedy and it's aftermath, you learn to live with failure. There is simply too much to handle. Each demand on your time steals from all the others. While you're failing at one thing, others fail from lack of attention. So you fail at those tasks, too, or do a poor job at them. Working your ass off—really working harder than you ever have in your life—running from one responsibility to the next and failing at all of them. It's discouraging.

This is some vicious game. I'm on the run now and the game is on. I'm not happy about it. I do it all for Robin. Any lesser cause than Robin and my whole life—what I had been building up until Louise died—by now I would have abandoned the whole thing by the side of the road.

I swear, I would be off somewhere looking for a new vehicle.

I think I broke my thumb the other day, banging it on the refrigerator. One of my fits of rage. What a jackass. Starting to get far enough away from the anger to see that it has a face. Amazing that you have to gauge your happiness on being less pissed off.

I had that first almost unrecognizable whiff of spring air today. The snow has melted down, brown patches of grass now visible on my front lawn for the first time in weeks. I went out running this morning and when I got home I saw a pair of squirrels playing on my front lawn (they live up in my sycamore, I think). I watched them chasing each other up and down a maple tree, watched them rolling around together on the ground until I concluded that it was a debauchery. Right there in front of me! The shameless little bastards. Those squirrels looked fat and confident, like they knew they were going to make it through another winter, the worst being past us.

I take that as an official sign of spring coming on. You take your signs where you can get them. There are plenty to see—signs—if you slow down, pay attention. This is an activity that gets you the label of a slacker. People stop paying attention to you. That's where you want to be.

All this time off—am I turning into a dropout? What am I going to do out there in the world? I'm not the greatest team player, is my problem. I'm not against the team, or what they're doing. I'm not anti-social or even asocial. I simply don't have the attention span for cooperative action. I become a drag on the whole thing. I just want my little task, to be left alone to work at it for a while. I'll come up with something good. Let me astonish them with my brilliance. I promise to take half-rations and not bother anyone.

When Louise was dying we decided that what you have to do, in such a situation, is to try to live your whole life in one day. In the evenings, after the baby was asleep, we would try to have a few minutes together. We would sit out on the driveway with a glass of wine and look for shooting stars. It always felt like the last evening of the whole world, like tomorrow would never come. This was good for us. Even in the middle of the worst of it, if we could get outside and just pause at the end of the day, rest together.

It felt complete. I want to try to continue that. If a day is a complete thing of itself, starting out new and ending in sleep, then it's a unique thing that deserves more attention be paid to it than what you can give, working away in your cubicle there, measuring it off as the man says in coffee spoons. So much measured, abstract, essentially useless activity. Too much running around, never catching up, not enough time to even think about what you're really doing. No time to even question it at all: that should tell you something right there.

It's a conspiracy we are all part of, guilty of. You're just spinning the wheel around because everyone else is doing it. Seems like you couldn't stop it even if you wanted to. Well, you can get off that wheel. I'm not advocating laziness—nor am I downplaying hard work. I'm just asking for a realistic pace, something intelligible, so you can see the progress of what you've done, see what's ahead, decide for yourself what comes next instead of somebody deciding for you. Exercise some freedom now, while you still can: there could be some bad thing out there stalking you.

If there was one thing that drew us together, kept us together—Louise and I—it was a shared aesthetic and an almost child-like insistence that reality was an intrusion, to be tolerated at best, and if it had to be dealt with then there were other people, more willing, more capable, who could take care of it, keep it off us, allow us to play.

She was a youngest child, precocious, with two big brothers. She probably learned at an early age that a razor-sharp wit and a head start were her only weapons against the torments of much bigger boys—which to them, the way big brothers are, only meant that she had a big mouth and could run fast. She played on her own much of the time (the way she told it), carving out ever-larger circles from her mother's skirt in her family's big old house, telling stories to herself, making up songs, imagining friends when she needed them—much the way our daughter plays now.

I never knew her father. He died when she was seventeen, long before I came onto the scene, but from the stories she told it is clear that he was affable and gregarious, a tall man, intelligent and methodical, a Southern-born gentleman who doubtless encouraged her sassiness and charm. I can almost see Louise as a child, bouncing on her father's knee, working him the way Robin works me now—the joy of it. She later charmed me, too, and in a way she worked that charm on everyone who loved her—not insincere or deceptive, not at all, but with that little hidden laughter and an air of conspiracy, like she knew the secret but the secret was lost, or fragile. Only to be tread upon lightly. Only to be hinted at.

She charmed people from a need to impress herself upon them indelibly—as a poem or a painting, as a rare and beautiful bird. She liked herself. She wanted people to know who she was.

Myself, growing up, I was insulated from any real harm by my sprawling, happy family and literally scores of relatives. It was so safe that you came to expect that everything was going to be alright, nothing could touch you. I was the seventh of eight children, way down there at the bottom of the food chain—a lot of people blocking for me and they hardly knew that I was even there. It was pretty free. I told Louise when her troubles started that I wished that both of our families, all of our friends, a hundred people or more, that all of us lived in the same big house and we could just fall back into them, let them hold us up, absorb the thing that was making her sick, shake it off in one collective, monstrous immune response—project it far off into space with a force of will to protect their own—and then set us back down and we all go on.

It doesn't happen that way. She was slowly taken away from us, against our will. We all went out with her as far as we could, as long as we could, but then she went over. It must be lonesome. We all have to go through it. I'm not as afraid anymore: knowing she did it, hoping she's still there, waiting. Hoping they're all there. There is no death wish. It's more like a movement. People don't really choose to die as much as they follow each other into it, out of love. Does love die? We'll see. That's all you're bringing with you. If it's not strong enough you're not going to make it through.

11

Did I do everything I could? That's a question that's going to haunt me. Did I comport myself well? For the longest while I rejected the question on the grounds that it wasn't about me. It was about Louise first, and then it was about Robin. I would have been ridiculous to sit around worrying about how it *looked* like I was handling myself.

That may have been true when Louise was sick and dying, but now that she's gone it *is* about me, and Robin. Things changed. For the longest time I had to convince myself that it didn't matter how I felt. It matters now. I'm going to need to feel good about myself again. I'm no good to Robin or anyone else feeling I failed Louise somehow. I've got regret pouring out of my shoes and doubtless always will, but I need something to feel good about, too.

People have expressed that I handled myself well, that I gave Louise someone to lean on, that I've done a good job raising our daughter. But I honestly don't know. People will say almost anything to bolster you up. Maybe they just feel sorry for you. Maybe they're glad it isn't them. Or they're frustrated because they see your ass hanging out there in the wind—they want to carry some of your burden for a while, but it's not for them to do. So they give you a kind word. It all helps.

All I know is I think by now I could spin stories in the White House. That's what I did—what I've continued to do—every day. I learned to put a spin on things, pronounce some battle cry or hopeful outlook, anything that would make it seem like the fight was still worth fighting, that this day was just the first of many future and better days and it all started here—the way out. And some of those days were horrible, too—some of those days were too bleak for any third-rate spin. I had to be good, and I usually was. I always came up with something to keep the wagons moving west. It was one thing I did provide. I know I did some good that way. I surprised even myself. People have known me as a bit of a smartass, frankly—cynical and wary. Turns out that was just cover, protection. I found out just how hopeful and optimistic I can be.

Where did that hope come from? It was there all along, I think, waiting for just such a crisis, hoping it wouldn't come, like a reserve coming up from deep below—bubbling up all the way from childhood, probably. All those happy, innocent times compressing down there under the weight of the years (now building up: I'm thirty-seven). A fine, black, heavy fuel—oil, or maybe diamonds down there at the bottom of it. And anyway who cares where it comes from? Don't question it. Just hope it doesn't dry up. Be thankful that it's there and use it. Keep drawing on it. If it runs out, fine. We'll discover some alternative fuel.

No, don't question, don't even for a minute stop to think. Thinking can only lead to panic. There's a hurricane ripping through your house, everything being tossed around and shattered, things blowing away, screaming, fear of oblivion. To panic, to voice or even entertain the notion of defeat, is to state the obvious and only raises doubt. You can doubt yourself later—and you will. File away that breakdown for when the storm has passed, for peacetime. That's why they call it *post*-traumatic stress. It may not be pleasant but at least it's something: Louise doesn't have a post-anything. So when it's going against you, and you've got nothing to draw on, draw on those reserves. Be responsible: use only what you need. A slow burn of the fuel. Some for now, some for later.

If a happy childhood is good for anything, it provides that touchstone, that very real place—it's not imaginary, you've been there, you *know* it's there—to which you will try to return when times get hard. Getting back to that innocence—that's what drives your hope. And I think I always knew something like these hard times would come. As a young man I tried to stay ready, tried not to get too high or too low, tried to acknowledge the fragile nature of the very good fortune I had experienced growing up.

Even as I was living it, I knew that there was something a little bit unreal—something almost too good, insulated, about my particular life in America in the late twentieth century. I even sought out some things to test myself. One summer during my college years a friend and I talked each other into joining the Marines. I fully expected to hate it, and I did hate it, mostly because it was hard. A romantic notion of proving my manhood is what compelled me, an almost unacknowledged need to find out if those oil reserves were there, if I had the fortitude to withstand a serious challenge.

I was exploring my character I guess, searching a little deeper than was otherwise necessary, simply to satisfy my mind that when things got rough—and they would get rough, eventually, I knew—that there was substance there to draw on and get me through. Drilling down in search of something not even defined. Geology of the soul. How much is there? What grade? How deep?

It was about developing some endurance, physical and mental, both together. I did not really want to be a soldier. The Marines were recruiting for officers, coming into the colleges and offering a chance to try out life in the Corps. A six-week paid vacation, they called it. You can walk away if you don't like it. No questions asked.

It was no vacation. A kind of glorified basic training is what it was. It was hot in Virginia that August, as I'm sure it is every August, and the humidity dripped like hot tar from the pale blue and limitless horizon. Even the American flag we saluted every morning at reveille and every evening at taps sagged on its pole like a wet rag at midday, heat radiating upward in liquid lines from the scorching black asphalt of the drill deck. We bunked in low-slung, fabricated steel Quonset huts that cooked us like roasting hens far out in those deep Southern woods. It was a remote place with an air of history. I imagined the men in blue and gray once gathered in places such as this and tasted fear in their mouths as the morning sun rose at Gettysburg or Antietam.

There were about three hundred of us, all around the age of twenty, college students, cockier than hell and more than happy to be doing something pretty crazy for our summer recess. Some of us admitted to one another in confidence that we were not really serious about joining the Marines. One guy told me he wanted to be a fashion model in New York, that he only joined the Marines to get in shape. But most of the guys were very serious—many had already been in the Marines as enlisted men, or had attended a military academy. They actually wanted to be Marine Corps officers, an idea I found both fascinating and repugnant. They harbored dreams of storming beaches with scores of men, of conquering the enemies of their country—of killing people.

The physical training was tough, pretty demanding, and I had a hard time keeping up. I'm athletic and was in good condition going in, but this was not about being an athlete. It was about being strong and having endurance. Most of the guys—"candidates" we were called—were in great shape. I was about average for sure, but I paced myself well, not feeling any need to distinguish myself. Several of the guys, really promising future officers, went too hard and burned themselves out. During the long training sessions there were candidates dropping all over the place with a variety of ailments: bad knees, allergies, heat exhaustion, asthma attacks. If anything went wrong, anything that might compromise their ability to train, they were sent home. About a quarter of the guys who started did not make it through.

Some of it was kind of fun—bivouacs in the deep forest, helicopter airlifts, crossing rivers on rope bridges, crawling around in the mud—we were boys playing army in the woods, which at bottom is probably what attracts men to that life. And although I struggled to keep up with the training, I figured out that they couldn't make you do anything you weren't capable of. I stuck back in the ranks and tried not to stand out in any way—which wasn't too hard.

The mental game was much harder. Psychologically it was excruciating: boring and tedious. After two weeks I was miserable and wanted to go home. The humiliation of actually quitting was the only thing that stopped me. There were some interesting guys in my platoon, guys from all over the country, but we were kept so busy maintaining our gear and attending classes (hours spent cleaning your weapon, two-hour classes on how to take a dump in the woods). There was rarely time for any conversation, much less any time to think—reflective thought being the last thing they wanted anyone engaging in. I did have a couple interesting late-night talks with one fellow, a student at NYU who drove a cab in the city. We discussed Sartre, who I hadn't read until he lent me one of his books. I read on my rack by flashlight after curfew, strangely desperate as I suddenly was for something of the mind, of weight, to counter the voluminous texts on personal hygiene and military protocol we were expected to memorize.

Mostly they kept us busy with plenty of banal tasks that had us feeling both rushed and stupefied. It wasn't hard to figure out the psychology of it: break them down, tell them they're dirt, then show them the new way, the Marine Corps way—the *right* way—then build them back up, make them feel a part of it. It wasn't all bad. I took a few things away from it. But I was a little lost and out of place certainly, sometimes desperately so, things turned upside down, waking up at three-thirty in the morning and stumbling out into the dark, setting off on a ten-mile forced march in full gear and a fifty-pound pack, realizing my buddies at home were probably just collapsing stone drunk into bed after a summer night's revelry.

They kept us confused—deliberately so, of course—and out of step, had us stand around in the hot sun for hours, dog-tired from lack of sleep, only to suddenly command that we had five minutes to get ready for inspection: boredom and panic, rushing around—hurry up and wait, as they say. Preparing you for the life, probably: where you'll wait for years perhaps and then suddenly find yourself thrown into action. You have to be able to make that instant transition. In battle, they taught us, time speeds up—heavy, compressed action, overload. You have to slow down your mind, think clearly, process, prioritize, make a decision. We were to be officers, after all, leaders of men in combat. You had to imagine yourself in that situation some-day: earth and sky exploding all around you—people trying to *kill* you—men with mothers, wives and sons looking at you for the signal, for the way out or through.

Before I even went down there, I was fairly sure I didn't want that life, and then I was absolutely sure. My attitude was not great—I was only trying to endure it. It showed. I was graded near the bottom of my class. I would have loved to succeed at it, dazzle them with my brilliance, and then walk away. But I wasn't that good. After a while I just wanted to finish, to know that although I hated it I would always be glad I had seen it through.

When I finished up that summer I went home as lean and locked down as I'll ever be in my life, looking a little silly with my crew cut and my clothes a little baggier than when I went in. The recruiters kept after me for a while, but I told them no thanks—"I mean *really* fellas, no thanks"—and finally they left me alone and I slipped back into my lazy undergraduate life.

The last thing I wanted to do was join the military and go fight wars, but I tried not to have an attitude about it. We need guys like that, but it wasn't for me. I'm just glad to have had that experience. I surprised myself to some degree with the sense of accomplishment I took from it. I learned that those reserves were there, if needed—and of course, many years later, they were—although basic training with the Marine Corps is a picnic compared to what we experienced when Louise was ill, when she was dying, and after. But what it taught me is that a miserable situation can be endured, that I could do it, and that I could maintain some composure while things were going badly. It helped to prepare me. Nobody ever wants any real trouble, but sooner or later it will find its way to you. It gives you confidence in life to know that you can take a beating like that, and get back up again. To prevail, however damaged you may finally be.

And although I'm here now, and starting to move on, Louise did not make it. I hate that. The only thing that could make it all worse is if the thing that killed her had ruined me. It got a piece of me, no question—a big piece. But it didn't ruin me. I've still got my mind, my home, my daughter—all intact. Maybe this is the brick I've been looking for. Maybe we can rebuild with this one hard truth.

12

When the cancer came back again—when it metastasized (one of the great ugly words)—that is when the bootheel started to really grind her down. Louise had been through six months of chemotherapy, which had been very difficult, especially with the baby present, but she was still strong and defiant and through it there was a sense that the poison was really a precaution, overkill. We were certain the surgery had gotten all of the tumor, and with the chemotherapy we were even more convinced that any rogue cells still inside her were surely choking upon themselves as the drugs cornered them.

Louise was so mentally strong. She loved wolves, and in her mind she envisioned the chemicals as a pack of white wolves patrolling her passageways, seeking out those last, lone, desperate invaders and taking them down: she closed her eyes and heard the howl, felt the thrill of the chase, took ravenous, vengeful pleasure in the ripping of flesh and the crack of bones. Her wolves would protect her, she was sure, and then afterward—weary, with bloody face and the satisfied pleasure of the hunt, they slept in the snow.

By Christmas her hair had grown back some: she was burr-headed, cute like a little boy, so she had it styled to be more like a woman and I loved it, the way it swept off her face, which was shining now, deeper pools coming forth. I told her I would never let her grow her hair long again. She had a few new scars and she could never have more children, but she was whole and she was mine: the nights, the sighs, things coming back to us again.

We had a little party at a local bar, invited all our friends and family, passed the hat around at the end. Louise was lit from within that night. She had bought herself a beautiful silk dress for the occasion. Robin came too, in her own new dress, and stayed for a while until she was whisked away so Louise and I could stay late.

Still, there were trips to the doctor. In spring she caught a cold. Routine chest X-ray. A week later she called me at work: the anxiety in her voice like the wail of a dog in the distant night. A spot on her lung—probably just scar tissue from her surgery, her doctor had offered. Another MRI should allay our fears. But I was more than worried. We were right back in the middle of it. There was a feeling of having almost slipped away in time. Now the jury was deliberating again. More tests, insurance company hassles, forms and procedures, waiting for results.

The paranoia: she had just caught her breath. A week or two passed. Growing more nervous as we waited. Black crows on the lawn, hopping, hunched like vultures. Was that thing still out there?

I was furious. I am not violent by nature, but I found myself having black, gothic fantasies of vengeance. I wanted to pummel on this beast, justice in my shoulder, arm, fist: a running start, plant square on the left foot, meat of thigh and hips into it full. A flying right cross, power of fist on the jaw and the sweet-sickening sound of cracked bone. And then that lone, hanging silent instant before the drop of weight inert and powerless to the dusty floor.

You're done. Drag this thing out of here. None of that here. No more.

Probably nothing more horrible then—that day in June. Waiting. A gray, sticky morning, a call coming maybe that day about the tests on her lung. I had brought work home so I could be there. That now-familiar, desperate, reaching, helpless feeling. We waited some more. I thought maybe if I stepped out to get some work done the call would come, and that if I wasn't there, somehow the news would be good: bad things following me, I was trying to lead them away from her. I threw my briefcase in my truck, left the number of a coffee shop for her in case the call came, told her to call me right away if it did.

I drove over to a nearby town, the sky hanging like glue. I hadn't even stepped inside the place when I heard the phone ring, saw the girl put her hand over the phone and look around. I was the only customer. Are you so-and-so? I took the phone, a weakening in my legs.

"Hello?" Knowing it would be her.

"Honey…?" Her voice so empty and lost I couldn't reach her.

"Oh, baby…no."

She somehow put the words together to make a sentence. "I have cancer in my lungs…"

"Oh God, sweetheart…Oh sweetie, hold on, I'll be right home."

And then how do you bridge the distance back to her fast enough? Onto the sidewalk, running, stomping past the shops, tears and wild venomous hatred at who knows who.

Here we go. It's going to go down.

Into my truck, tight corners in the parking garage, wanting speed—a straightaway—wanting to rip that metal loose, hear the engine blow through the hood. Now a red light, slamming the steering wheel with my open hand. *Raging*.

"Goddammit! You motherscratchers!"

Talking to whom?

"You motherscratchers why? Why why why why why you motherscratchers why!?"

Imagining not God but some Council. Shaking my head at the audacity of their verdict, this fate.

"You muckity mucks. You motherscratching mucks. Why!?"

Somebody in the car next to me at the intersection, looking at me raving and crying out. The thing in there with me, not in there with them—so indiscriminate. They have no idea, they can only wonder. Green light. I rumbled down the road, almost looking for somebody to hit, pulled up, ran to our back door, leapt up the steps and into the kitchen. She was there. She was not some apparition. She was still there—warm and vulnerable. I embraced her with my whole body and soul, tried to fuse into her I held her so hard. I wanted to save her, wanted to *be* her. Something pulling us apart—actually feeling the gnashing and ripping away of her from me. The awful sound of it. And a pain you can't locate.

If there is a God—and there is much evidence to the contrary—why would we believe in Him? He casts us out here without our permission, abandons us when we need Him most. Some say God is love but I contend that we are love. We came up with it ourselves. There was a need and we filled it. Face it—the world He prepared for us is cold, unpredictable, unfeeling. We build a little fire with our love, it lasts a little while, and then the world puts it out. So we build another little fire, and so on. That's not faith. That's just taking direct action. Love is not a gift from God—that is too easy, that cheapens it. Love is our invention: it is heroism against preposterous odds. God doesn't have anything to do with it. Those who give Him credit are fools.

As are those who think God is punishing them for something. It takes a true hatred of self to come up with a concept like Original Sin. Or the work ethic. These are just fairy tales. Keep people in line. Keep them *working*. Somebody once said beware the man of one book. People so dumb they deserve whatever they get. God may at some time reveal himself as much smarter than He looks, but for now we can only conclude that he is either dead, inept, or off working on some new experiment, trying to get it right this time. Blasphemy my stinking arse. Say whatever the hell you want. God cannot punish you any more than He can help you. He just watches. We amuse Him.

Or if He does love us, He's got an interesting way of showing it. He's got a lot to explain. I will be interested to hear that story. If we must have a God, let's hold Him accountable, too. Confession should be a *dialogue*. Let's all come clean.

Can I get myself into trouble talking this way? I sincerely doubt it. I can starve myself worshipping Him, I can pray to Him until my knees are bloody, and nothing happens. Wife still suffers. Wife dies. Daughter has no mother—looks at me and asks me why. I feel like that old man in the Python movie, right before they stone him for even daring to utter God's name—at this point, what difference does it make? "Jehovah! Jehovah! Jehovah!" I cry.

And I don't want to hear about His law. It is our law. We came up with it to keep from killing one another over the spoils on this God-forsaken place. I try to love my fellow men because I feel sorry for the poor bastards—I see myself in them.

Meanwhile, from possibly sealing my seat in Hell, I turn to shit. Robin is constipated. Thank…um…*God*, she is in roaring good health in all other ways. We're working on it. Endless pursuit of the perfect crap. It comes eventually, but not quietly: it is preceded by discussion, cajoling, strategy. Laying out the maps on the table in search of a steady, unspectacular dump.

She's so beautiful, so good-natured and naturally prone to happiness, but I'm naïve to think it all has not gotten to her somehow. She is just waking up to it as I try to sleep. Though she cannot be mistaken that I adore her, I'm sure she also has seen the cracks in my fragile patience, sees how poorly I disguise the extra burden I feel in trying to rein it all in. And yet she knows how heavily she relies on me, makes no allowance for any other possibility.

I am true north on her compass. Of course from birth, and for a long time, Robin reached first for Louise. But then somewhere in those last months before Louise died, Robin's care was completely passed on to me. Suddenly it was always me who came when she cried in the night, who bathed her and fed her, who tucked her in and sang for her at bedtime, whose voice she heard first in the morning. I find it hard to imagine how that was for both of them—that handoff, the letting go.

Such a terrible loss right out of the gate: it's going to be tricky trying to raise Robin out of this tragedy. And I won't settle for just survival—I want her to be happy. I want her to prosper, have courage and love her life and figure out how to get what she wants, how to hold onto it when she does find it. Losing her mother can never be a good thing for her, but maybe it can give her some depth to draw on later, some knowledge of the deeper mysteries that many people do not encounter until they're older, if at all.

Or, it could be something that weighs her down. It's my job to see that doesn't happen. I want her to understand it fully, to feel the loss and the sorrow and the terrible void, and I want her to learn to put it aside. We talk about it often. She gets sad and tells me she misses her mother, and I tell her that's alright: I miss her too.

And she knows how much more she depends on me now. The other day Robin said: "I don't want you to die for a long, long time Daddy, because I'll miss *you*, too." Such fear and sadness in a little girl, but oddly it sustains my hope in a way, because it's evidence of that courage she is going to need. It must be hard for her to confront that sadness, to voice it. That is a rare and honest quality—pure natural ability. That's all her. I've got to encourage that kind of spirit, help it grow. Life is longer and more difficult than she can even imagine now, but if she can endure all of this, learn to see past it, then maybe she really can be stronger and better for it. I need to help her see that long view. "I'm not going to die for a long, long time darling," I told her. "And you won't die for a long, long time after that. Then you and me and Mommy can all be together. But we've got a lot of life to live first. We've got to do our best to be happy."

By necessity, I think, she seems to have come up with a powerful *reason* to be happy. It courses through her. She has the bounce, literally. This big thing that could weigh her down and she keeps bouncing. Her legs are powerful, her energy kinetic and constant. At times you can't stop her from bouncing. If she ever begins to crap on a regular basis she'll be knocking her skull on the ceiling. We express our anger around here, too. It upsets things for a while but ultimately is better than a sniffle, a sigh, and a little quiet acceptance. The visceral must be met with the visceral, however it is expressed. Save your stoicism for things that are smaller than you.

We're at war with our bodies. We love them, but they fail us. Beautiful machines that ultimately fall apart. We mistake them for ourselves—they are not. Your body is not yourself—see the way it feels everything indiscriminately, nothing being headed off at the gate, everything just flowing through, all of the good and bad. You would never have the courage, or the wisdom, to allow for that.

It's a gamble—the decision to become human, a thrill ride we can't resist. All these sensual delights: our bodies just a way for us to touch them, conjured up from the dust by our very minds to reach out. We commit ourselves to them and live with the consequences. What a masterpiece, the human body, the way it knows what's good for us despite ourselves, the way it knows we need to feel everything.

Maybe that's it. Maybe we really did choose to live, back in our time before living—fully knowing what we were up against. Maybe Louise chose. Maybe she knew her fate, or even designed it herself. Some test, or some problem she needed to work out. Maybe if there is a God and He has a plan—maybe that is His plan. If that is the case, then I retract all blasphemy. Retract it all on the grounds of ignorance. A merciful God will understand.

Anyway I think I'm entitled to shoot my mouth off a little. I'm getting my ass kicked around here and I'm only trying to stick up for myself.

13

It can no longer be ignored. Last night another nightmare involving water. I have them more and more—some in waking hours, some in sleep. Nightmares of being pulled under in deep water, of floodwaters rising, of being stranded on a tiny boat in a terrible storm far out to sea. Other people have them too, I'm sure. Water is a powerful symbol. Life came from water, little creatures floating happily there for eons before they ever thought to crawl upon the land. We came from the sea, our ancestral home. It calls to us in dreams. Some I remember so vividly that clearly there was something being communicated, something realized.

The first, a waking nightmare, framed squarely now in my mind between the two infinite edges of a long, green, dusty summer. I was twelve. I stood on the starting block, nervous with anticipation and dread. I had not lost a race all summer, but the boy on the block next to mine was an ace. Word had gotten around. His best time beat mine by less than a second. I took my mark. This was for supremacy in the league, supremacy of the whole world for all I knew. Fifty meters fly. Two swimmers and the delicious air of an August evening.

The gun went off. I hit the water and after two huge, powerful strokes all my strength was gone. I was over-stoked. My coach had been in my ear all day trying to pump me up. I put it all into those first two strokes, wild, not in rhythm. When I rose for my first breath I swallowed down about half the pool, found myself choking violently and treading water in the middle lane as the other boy churned with the ease of a porpoise toward the far wall. Two hundred people crowded around the pool and all eyes on me as I flopped and splashed: choking, in every sense of the word.

After a few moments of mortification there I caught my breath and decided the race was lost, broke stroke and free-styled with slow humiliation toward the turn. Ahead I could see my coach kneeling at the water's edge and waiting. When I started to climb out of the pool he told me to get back in the water and finish the race.

Gently he said this. And how do you figure a coach? Not only did I not want to finish the race, I never wanted to swim again. I wanted to disappear or be someone else. All those people watching, the other team cheering for their guy, me having let my team down, my mother and father and friends somewhere in the crowd. As badly as I wanted this nightmare to end I saw that the pool was the only place where I could hide for a few seconds more.

So I pushed off and started swimming again, decided what the hell if I'm going to swim it I may as well do the proper stroke. That was one tired and feeble butterfly, my form terrible by the time I brought it home. The other boy had already climbed out of the pool. His time was absolutely smoking. He would have beaten me anyway, I figured. I never could have touched that time.

Another nightmare came in sleep, many years later. I was a young man, and my brother and a friend of ours and I were all out paddling around in a big, lazy river in some fashion of paddle boats. There were others out on the water with us, people with garlands of flowers around their necks, wearing Hawaiian shirts and colorful hats, all of us paddling about and mingling and making merry: a huge, floating cocktail party. Our boats had holders for our drinks and trays for food. We would paddle ashore to the bar to refill our drinks and load up on sandwiches and chicken salad, then paddle back out to the revelry in the middle of the river, everyone whooping it up and having a great time.

Only my boat was slowly sinking. As hard as I paddled I could not get my boat to float up on the surface like the others. Instead it listed and dipped below the slow-moving surface of the water. The gentle waves lapped up and splashed over the edges of my boat, spoiling my drink and making my sandwiches soggy. I tried to call out to my brother and friend but no sound came forth, and anyway they were too far away to hear me now, too absorbed in the party to even notice me struggling madly to right my boat. They were having no such trouble. They paddled about effortlessly, their boats sitting high and dry up out of the water. They were having a great time of it.

A third nightmare, again in waking hours. My family had gathered for our annual autumn weekend near a cold, clear lake way up north, the burning reds and yellows of the season spreading out in all directions, a redemptive breeze blowing down from Canada at the end of a dry, stifling summer. Robin was still a baby, and Louise was just finishing up six months of chemotherapy. She was sick and exhausted and hadn't wanted to come, but she knew I had been looking forward to this trip for months. In the end she decided she could just as easily feel awful beside a cool lake as she could at home. We packed up the baby's things, whistled the dog into the car, and drove north.

I was glad to be going on this trip. A long, peaceful, solo canoe ride had been on my mind all summer—a chance to float and drift on those restorative waters. When I saw my chance one afternoon that weekend, I pushed a suspicious-looking aluminum boat into the water and, breaking about five rules of boating safety, wobbled unsteadily into the surprisingly stiff current of the narrow, strait-like lake.

Louise had come down to the dock to see me off, the baby in her arms, and she looked at me with a combination of envy and concern as I paddled out past a little point and steered the boat into the current. I stayed close to shore for a while, and then cut directly across the mouth of a little bay. It was a beautiful afternoon, the sun shining and the fall colors reflecting off the fish-scale waters. Just what I needed, I recall thinking. Even better than I had imagined.

I was about halfway across the bay when the boat tipped. The water was cold in early October, of that I am certain, but strangely I don't recall noticing that as I quickly ran through a succession of ill-fated and thoroughly wrong-headed attempts to get myself out of this mess without any further embarrassment. First I righted the canoe and tried to climb back in, but something told me that a boat listing sideways and half-full of water was not the safest place to be. Next I swam a little ways off and plucked a life jacket out of the water and tried to put that on, only to discover at this most inopportune moment that it is virtually impossible to tie on a life jacket in such a situation. As my heavy clothes and waterlogged shoes made treading water extremely difficult, I learned in the worst possible way that a life jacket does nobody any good unless they are wearing it *before* they hit the water.

After struggling with that for longer than I probably should have, and after giving one final consideration to the humiliation I would surely endure—and the expense I was undoubtedly racking up—for having sunk a canoe at the bottom of the lake, I decided the smartest thing to do now would be to swim for shore. It didn't look too far and I'm a strong swimmer. After a number of wrongheaded decisions the sensible thing finally did win out. *Don't screw this up any further son, just get to shore and then figure out how to salvage the canoe.*

After two strokes the panic set in. I was suddenly very tired. After all the struggling by the boat, and with the weight of my wet clothes—a heavy sweatshirt, jeans, boots—curiously, some very bad thoughts started to sink into my mind. My arms suddenly felt heavy and useless, almost paralyzed. And the shore looked far. How far? I wondered. Fifty yards? A hundred? Under different circumstances this would have been an easy swim, but I was quickly growing very, *very* tired.

Then came the first realization that I might actually be drowning. For one lucid moment I saw the little one-paragraph item in the newspaper: *A thirty-five-year-old man drowned Saturday on a small inland lake when his canoe capsized in twelve feet of water*...I was actually reading the newspaper report of my own death. I wanted to swim, but I didn't feel like I was going anywhere.

I stepped outside myself. This is exactly how it happens, I thought. How many times had I read that story in the newspaper and it had been someone else? Why couldn't it be me this time? The whole year had been such a struggle and now it had finally caught up with me, now it was ready to pull me under. Is this what you want? I asked myself. And perhaps the only redeeming development in the whole debacle came in response to that question—nothing. No answer, no hesitation. No mulling it over. I just started swimming. Swim for Robin, I told myself. Just swim hard and strong and never stop swimming.

And soon I was swimming again, a few strokes, a look up to see that the shore was indeed coming closer, a few more strokes. Breathing heavily, my arms like hundred-pound weights. And I thought of Louise, all she had been through: surely I could swim a little more.

Pretty close now. Should I try to touch bottom? Feeling if the bottom wasn't there I might never come back up. I had to try for it. I extended my foot downward and felt for sand. There it was. I was standing on the bottom, my head just above water.

I looked around. Neat little cottages painted up in cheerful whites, yellows, and blues all around the bay, most of them closed down for the winter, their windows like hollow eye sockets staring out impassive and lonesome upon the scene. Boat-lifts and docks pulled ashore for the season, a weather-beaten flag waving easily among a stand of sugar maples and birches. All silent. Nobody had witnessed this struggle. I could have gone down and nobody would have seen.

I looked back at the canoe, half-submerged, and the wreckage of oars and life jackets floating nearby. That was close, I thought. It wasn't real close, but it was close enough to feel the breath of it. Amazing, the speed of it, the nearness. One slip-up and death can be on top of you before you even realize.

Or how about a thousand slip-ups, you dumbass? As I walked up to the road and made the half-mile trip back to our little stand of cottages, I didn't know whether to feel relieved or humiliated. I was sure to be ribbed about this little stunt for years to come: that was to be expected. But as I walked, water dripping off my clothes, down my face, squeezing out of my shoes—a little chill coming over me now in the freshness of the season—I also began to see that I had almost bought it out there. How stupid would that have been? What a waste. What awful timing. My family needing me and I'm off in some tin-can canoe trying for a Hallmark moment.

And the thought crossed my mind: maybe I actually *was* dead. Maybe my body was still back there bobbing white as a turnip on the glassy surface of the lake. I was a ghost now. I heard sirens wailing far down out on the county highway. Could I actually be dead? As I walked the little road leading into our resort it occurred to me that this was as likely as anything else. I had never been dead before. Perhaps this was what it was like. Perhaps when I got back to my family nobody would see me or hear me. I would stand among a group of them screaming *look at me, I'm right here.* But they would go on with what they were doing. Somebody might ask, "Has anyone seen Dave? He's been gone a long time." And I would find out that way: I was a dead man walking the earth like a character in some awful *B* movie.

I heard the spin and crunch of car wheels coming up the gravel road behind me. I turned and recognized my sister's car. Good, I thought, she'll see me and stop and then I'll know. I'll have to explain the whole thing to her but at least I'll know. And what is it with all those sirens? My sister's car approached, going *a little bit too goddamn FAST* as far as I was concerned. Yes, that's her I said to myself. Terrific, let's get this matter settled.

And she blew right past.

She never even saw me. I stood there by the side of the narrow drive, soaking wet, looking right at her, and she drove on past never once even turning her head. That's it, I thought. I'm dead! Those sirens are for me and I drowned and this is how it is: I'm a ghost, I'm dead. Walking a bit faster now. I came into the clearing and saw a big group of people sitting in lawn chairs farther down near the lake. Am I actually dead? Still not really believing it, still on the fence, it could go either way.

I was starting to get cold. I'll just slip into my cabin here first, I thought, and dry myself off and change my clothes before I head down there. They will see me or they won't. I'll find out the truth, but if I'm dead for all time I would like to be dry for it.

I reached down and picked up an apple, and it felt like an apple. A good sign. Sirens blasting right past on the main road. Somebody had obviously seen my half-sunken canoe.

Standing up I saw one of my older brothers look up from his book under a shady tree. Me shifting cold and stupidly there like a wet dog pondering an apple. His half-bemused expression told me all I needed to know. He shook his head and went back to his reading. "What the hell happened to *you?*"

All *snide* he was. As though it had long been known that there was something wrong with me and here was further proof.

A fourth nightmare that came in sleep. Robin and I were with a large group of people trying to escape an island. Thousands of people, an exodus. Nighttime, we could see the lights of the mainland far off. All the people in haste, something gaining on us, people plunging into the roiling surf and heading off in a long column toward the lights of the shore, the way being pointed by a narrow band of green light, like a path, emanating from deep beneath the surface. I hesitated. Robin does not swim, but we would have to go anyway. I found a large foam board. Robin climbed atop it and I pushed off into the surf, kicking hard with my legs as I steadied Robin on the board in front of me.

I saw how the sea leveled off out past the breakers. I told Robin to hold on as we rode up and over the first wave, felt the salt water in my eyes, tasted it, crying out *hold on!* as the next wave came up and we crashed through and soon we were in a column with the others, the sea calmer and the water actually buoyant now as great buttressing bubbles of air and a strange light churned up yellow-green from some source below.

I pushed the board forward and kicked hard, felt good and strong as we fell in line with the other swimmers. We were going to make it. Only where was Robin? Gone! She was no longer up on the board. I turned and swam back furiously, calling her name, sure she had gone under. Knowing I could not bear this, never this.

People swam past methodically, not hearing me or not caring, worrying about themselves, the water bubbling up iridescent and carrying them along. I called for Robin, my heart heavy with thousand pound steel balls of sadness pulling me under and me ready to go under, all of it having been so hard and always the fear that only this or something like this could make it worse and now it was happening.

And then I saw her. She had fallen behind, but she was swimming on her own amid the column of swimmers heading toward the black and distant shore. She was tired and struggling with it, but she had done it, had kept herself afloat until I could find her.

I awoke and felt my heart slowly return to its normal size and weight, rose from bed and went down the stairs. There she was, softly sleeping and breathing like a small bird in the light from beside her bed. I pulled the covers aside and eased in and curled gently beside her and we both slept.

III

Fire

14

In a few days Robin and I are flying down to Florida, with my brother and his wife and their two girls, to visit my mother and father, who are now retired and spend the rough part of the winter down south. This has been a strange, harsh winter already and I'll be happy for the break. Robin is giddy with excitement, asks me to paint a dream of Florida for her every night before she goes to sleep. I try to imagine her anticipation: she's going to get into a time machine and be transported to some magical, warm, green place with an ocean, with fish and birds and fire ants and Grandma and Grandpa.

It's been hard keeping us both calmed down about it. People in the South can never understand the thrill we Northerners feel, leaving behind all this cold and damp, literally ascending above it in our liberating jetliner, piercing that oppressive layer of heavy, gray clouds into the bright sunlight—the first time we've seen sunshine in *weeks* sometimes, I swear. And when we walk off that airplane the transformation is sublime, the sudden rush of green, scent of flowers and grasses, the narcotic air. It really is almost science fiction: time travel, the length of a daydream and we're there.

We're tired—Robin and I. We need this trip. There's been some hard work going on around here. Mental work I mean, healing. I certainly haven't been doing any home improvements. I think my house is falling apart. For three weeks in January the winter weather was as bad as it gets around here. Deep cold and snow heavy on the roof. The cold beats on the house: everything stiffer, things contracting, opening up, cracks developing. Winter loosens things that way. And it is so quiet. You're forced to live with yourself a little more: listen to the creaking sounds in your bones, realize the same things are prying you loose, too.

Nature is so vexing, so seductive and teasing, when it falls asleep. It always comes back and yet you doubt: you are not convinced. People begin talking to themselves. "Will spring *ever* come?" they'll ask of no one in particular, standing in the checkout line at the supermarket. In the very depth of winter you'll find yourself wondering if maybe this year the spring won't come at all: the snow and ice will keep coming right into July, August, September. It will confound the scientists, send them to their charts and instruments and satellites in search of answers. And they'll find nothing: it just got cold and stayed cold. No explanation. It could happen, you say to yourself. This whole state was once leveled flat by a glacier.

You want the proof, the feeling of that first southerly breeze, the smell of grass and the earth waking up. Every year it surprises us. One day the temperature climbs above sixty. Neighbors you haven't seen in months come outside in their shirtsleeves to walk their dogs or push a stroller. "Sixty degrees!" they'll say. "It's amazing!" Apparently they doubted it too.

Here, the clouds descend upon us around early November and don't really lift again until April, if we're lucky. That's a long period of waiting and doubt. We try to hide from it, to carry on inside our reasonable minds as though we were not natural beings. But even holed up in your house, with your television and computer and climate control, Nature plays on your longings. From the depth of winter you long to wake up, breathe, grow. At your base you are no more complex than a plant, are victim to the same cycle of living and dying. Nature gives birth to you, hypnotizes you, then just leads you around. You don't even have to do anything. Just fall for it. You're under the spell.

Louise hated these gray, deep, long winters. She was like a tropical flower, delicate and temperamental the way she reached out toward the sun—the way she retracted from the cold and darkness. I had always enjoyed our winters, or at least met them with the standard Midwestern defiance, but each year I was with Louise she pulled me a little more toward her way of seeing things. I teased her that she ruined winter for me. Now the winters pass with more difficulty: so heavy and oppressive, this blanket of clouds, ice, and silence. We're forced to shut down, to wait. It's almost as though we're meant to sleep through it, like bears, or seeds in the ground.

For our honeymoon we knew we wanted to visit a Caribbean island. Louise planned the whole thing: read the guidebooks, researched the different islands, started a little fund to save money for it, even picked the place finally—St. Kitts, in the British Virgin Islands. After our wedding reception, we stayed up all night carousing with friends in a hotel until a limousine came at four in the morning to take us to the airport. I promptly fell asleep in the car and more or less did not wake up until several hours later, when Louise poked my arm as the plane circled above St. Kitts. I woke up from the greatest evening of my life to the sight of that happy, mountainous isle, sitting like some huge, mythical, moss-covered stone amid the blue-shimmering Caribbean waters far below. I was so happy it was hard to tell when the dream had started, or if or when it had ever stopped.

On the ground we hailed an open-air taxi to take us to our villa. As we drove the two-lane highway through the island's interior, past sugar cane fields stretched out under the blazing sun, the driver smiled and sang a tune that was locally popular at the time:

Sugar pumpkin, sweet dumplin'
Ooooohhh, let me tell you something!
You've been on my mind,
For a very long time,
Yes a very long time...

Almost instantly we melted into island life as though we were coming home. Louise's face blossomed into a smile as though she were native to that place: she flourished there, amidst the sun and wind and the blue of the sea, the perfume of flowers, the rich smell of heat and earth and the green hills. She reached some sort of completion on St. Kitts, I think—it was only three months later that she became pregnant and soon the troubles began. She was never more beautiful to me. Her skin—she was very fair, and she took pains to protect it—it seemed to absorb the light and shine back as though lit from underneath, soft and deep and white as the low, lazy clouds hovering above the simmering volcano that had birthed the island ages ago. Her eyes twinkled back at the dappling sea, blue and shining, intense and searching—mysteries in both woman and water, far beneath.

It was now off-season on St. Kitts, most of the other tourists had gone home, and the grateful locals were every day slipping further into "island time," that easy, slow-moving, liquid way about them as they looked forward to the long, quiet summer ahead. We arrived at our resort before noon, had a tall tumbler of the local rum punch on the terrace, then checked in. A young man carried our bags up to our little villa on the hillside, and we sent him back with the television. We opened every window to let in the breeze, drew the blinds to create a cool half-darkness, and made love for lunch like half-starved children, surprising ourselves at the appetite we had been building for each other. After, we slept lightly as the breezes blew in, the strange music of exotic birds above in the trees.

That first afternoon Louise had her hair braided on the beach. She sat at a small picnic table under the palms as a large, ebony-skinned woman slowly wove and twisted her fine chestnut hair, stringing in beads of green and sparkling blue. Two or three local women sat and watched, the group of them conversing in that strange, happy, musical dialect—about every third word something you can recognize—Louise with her eyes closed, smiling, listening intently. She was stunning, simple, at ease in this place, wrapped in colorful sarongs, white cotton shirts, barefoot, smelling of jasmine oils and salt.

We passed the time lazily, conscious of every passing moment. It was a perfect feast, and we consumed it slowly.

Our villa sat just a little way up the hill above the sea. Behind us the hill was skirted with red and yellow flowers and—further up—plantain trees, jungle, monkeys. The monkeys would come down to feed on the fruit trees. Out walking, you could catch them sneaking around behind you if you paid attention. Tiny lizards flitted across the patio, stray kittens wandered through the gardens, all freely coming in and out of our rooms, all the doors and windows open, everyone—everything—breathing.

We made friends with a few other couples, took day trips as a group to other parts of the island. We saw the old fort— Brimstone Hill—on a high hill at the southern tip. Like every other habitable place in the New World, St. Kitts had changed ownership several times during the colonial era. The British and French took turns throwing each other off the rock, and each conqueror made improvements to the fortifications. The fort is surrounded by rings of stone wall as you ascend the hill, and at the top there are cannons aimed out into the passive blue sea.

Standing up there, absorbing the history of that piece of ground, it's almost absurd really—to think of those pale, thick Europeans in their heavy coats and boots, rolling their boulders, lugging all their iron to the top of that fresh green paradise. To see them digging in—mercenary soldiers with no stake in the fortunes being carried off the island—setting it all up like some stone London slum, slopping their meat and potatoes, sweating out last night's rum in the brilliant heat. And then, with the attack, frightened, tasting their fear in the rising dust, bayonets high as the invaders scaled the walls, they clashed metal in the glint of sun, brilliant flashing of sharpened steel, blood running into the ground as the enemy fell back again like a wave into the sea. Only to return again.

Nobody can own a place like this. It belongs to everyone, and no one. It is a secret. Whoever would give up the secret, claim paradise as his own, send his brute, drunken mercenaries to pilfer it from the world—he brings some kind of demon with him, from outside, from back in his cold, distant home. I know I would not trust myself with the ownership of such a place. I have done a little traveling and I have seen paradise—it is still here in places, though remote, you have to work to find it—and each time I saw it there arose within me a strange vertigo. The sensual explosion in such a place is so powerful that it overcomes me, forces me to lose my ground. Here was the world as it was before time, before consciousness itself—so much older and wiser and more beautiful than any name we could give it. We reduce things to understand them, but beauty such as this is something beyond our ability to contain it, like a wild animal—impersonal, almost extinct. The power in paradise lies in its utter indifference to us. We can visit, but only graciously. Leaving no trace, we must return to our homes. The moment we make a claim upon it we lose it.

Perhaps I simply feel unworthy of paradise. While Louise spontaneously and completely opened herself to the beauty of the place, I was more guarded, not fully trusting. Perhaps—coming from this cold, dark, industrial city in the northern Midwest—I was simply illuminated in this bright, soft place for who I am, and I shuddered at the hard edges, saw the build-up and grit, the armor. I knew that in my short stay in paradise I could not possibly scrub all of that grit away. It would require more time, months or more likely years, to settle into the ease of the place, to lubricate the joints, relax the smile, achieve the sway of palm branches or the freshness of salt air that has blown in over miles of lavender seas. And so I resisted a little, held myself back nervously, knowing I would need all that armor again when we returned home.

If I was looking for an omen or a foreshadowing of what would soon descend upon our lives, I would have to consider that it all started right there, on that beautiful tropical island, that Eden. Though Louise and I had been together for several years, it was finally with our wedding that we felt truly as one. There was a sense, for both of us, that all the last seeds of doubt were gone, that this was the final commitment and now something new, a new entity altogether—a family of two—had been created.

It caught me off guard, both the sudden feeling of permanence and the sense of happiness it afforded. I'm certainly guilty of taking things too casually at times, but I found that our long engagement and traditional wedding did what they were supposed to do—made us realize that this was an important step in our lives, one that could not easily be undone. I was dragged along reluctantly through much of the process—the wedding showers, the planning, families coming together to meet—but I found myself more drawn into it as we went along.

At first I was simply slow in warming to the idea of marriage at all—and I don't really know why. I knew I loved Louise, but I have always had a problem with committing to one thing when it entails closing doors that lead to others, however remote. Getting married is a milestone, and once you've arrived at it you're really forced to leave a part of yourself behind—part of you dies to be honest about it. It must.

Eventually all the flak and social pressure—real or imagined—that I was getting from Louise and our friends and families wore me down. I had held out a long time, made a noble stand for procrastinators everywhere, but eventually I caved. When in doubt, do the right thing.

It started with the engagement ring. I really was making very little in salary at the time and had no savings. I could have gotten away without buying an expensive ring. If anything it seems more popular now to dispense with tradition and do something practical. But in the end and despite most evidence to the contrary I am an incurable though understated romantic. I felt a need to rise to the moment. I wanted to surprise Louise and strangely felt compelled to spend way more than I could afford. I had heard stories of people doing the practical thing. Usually it just ended up sounding calculated or lame. Or cheap.

Or even worse, theatrical—I could have pictured Louise and I planning some cute production. We would shop for a ring together, make dinner reservations at some expensive restaurant, cue the violins, call for champagne at the big moment, involve fifty innocent diners in our melodrama. The preparations could never be too detailed: (Would the *maitre d'* be so kind as to capture it all on this video camera?)

Somehow I don't think I could have coaxed Louise through that kind of spectacle—we would have both been throwing up our Linguine Bolognese by the end of it. And then she would have refused me.

Some couples, after much enlightened discussion, will reject the whole notion of an engagement ring as chauvinistic and archaic altogether, a sign of ownership, the sense of property being traded back and forth ("How much for the little girl?"). Too cerebral if you ask me. Also very socialist, and socialists God bless 'em are the cheapest bastards of them all.

Do something *practical* with your money seems to be the growing sentiment—pay off a few credit card debts, buy some new living room furniture. Well that just sucks. Dreary, miserable, proletarian. Once you've graduated from school there are few occasions left that call for the grand and utterly useless gesture. Asking the love of your life to marry you seems to qualify. Get a nice ring, I told myself, nice enough to where it hurts. Make a sacrifice. It symbolizes everything you've got.

One day while contemplating this I began to look at my car—my very practical, proletarian, four-door economy car—and I put it up for sale. I cashed the check from the sale, walked into a jewelry store and laid down more money than I had ever held in my life. My hands were sweating, and I felt oddly alone, as though I was doing something I could never take back. I walked out of there holding the little black case as though it contained the last of a rare species of bird—I didn't even know what to do with it—and then I had to call somebody for a ride home.

When I got there I promptly hid the ring deep in a drawer as though that bird might fly. I'm going to wait for the right *moment*, I explained to myself. It stayed hidden there for nearly four months.

The moment finally came on a warm spring evening as we were getting ready for a symphony concert. I had wanted it to happen spontaneously. I really do loathe contrivance I guess—I was waiting until I felt all the stars were in alignment. I knew it would come eventually. We were having a glass of wine before heading out for the evening, dressed up nice, Louise in a very elegant black dress. I thought to myself: Isn't this perfect?

Before I knew what was happening I had bounced up out of my chair and was digging around in my dresser, trying to find that little black case—hoping it was still there as I hadn't looked at it in months. I took a little peek inside, curious myself because I had forgotten what the ring looked like, and when I sat down she was completely unaware, still sitting at our dining room table, the supple, fragrant air of a spring evening breathing in and out with the flap of lace curtains as though that room were the lungs of the world.

She was smiling as I sat down. We were both excited. We had planned to have dinner at a nice restaurant in the city, and later the symphony would be performing Beethoven's *Pastoral* on that pastoral spring evening.

"What are you smiling about?" I asked.

She said nothing, just blinked both eyes at me the way she did. She shook her hair and laughed, her earrings jingling. Fresh air and perfume about the room. I placed the black case upon the table. She looked at it, puzzled, began to form the words in her mind to ask what it was. Only before she could finish the thought a color like peach blossom swept across her cheeks and the waters came up to her eyes.

"Are you happy?" I asked her.

And she said "Oh…"

I opened the case and pulled out her ring. I looked at it again. My car for a ring? Yes, everything I have for that ring. It could never be beautiful enough to speak for me.

"Louise Mooney." I said. "Darling. Will you marry me?"

And she was crying when she kissed me, when she said yes.

The breaking of such a fusion of two souls can only be wrought with the most uncommon pain, and when I think back over the long history of that breaking, I can only wonder that perhaps the first fissure developed on St. Kitts, a place that seemed so like heaven that perhaps it began calling her there. Perhaps a little part of her began to listen, was hypnotized or transfixed by the promise of some unknown, far off, better place. And perhaps in my refusal to give myself over fully, in my reluctance to fully trust the seductions of that paradise, a little part of me began to pull back. Perhaps in our opposite pullings a tiny, imperceptible crack developed, and some demon took that as an opportunity.

In fact I met the Devil there, on St. Kitts—or at least a guy who called himself by that name. The bar at our resort was a round, open-air cabana out near the beach, not forty feet from where the little breakers tickled the shoreline. The resort was set in a cove, back in under the evening shadow of Monkey Hill—and the beach began at the base of those cool cliffs, then stretched off seemingly forever from there like a soft yellow road.

The Monkey Bar was popular with locals, ex-pats, other tourists, a collection of different faces gathering every late afternoon to drink the fine local beer, listen to the happy island music, and watch the evening blues deepen over the water. Louise and I would go down there for a drink before going out to dinner, and sometimes made it back, later, for dancing and fun, the crowd and the volume of the music having grown exponentially while we were gone.

The Devil was from Iowa. He was big and muscular, with floppy blond curls and a sunburned face. He told me he worked construction on some villas that were being built nearby. In fact we could see the site from our seats at the bar—half-constructed stucco walls blushing pink in the twilight on a hill above the sea. We talked briefly one afternoon, sitting around the bar, and it was odd when we discovered that not only did we have the same name, we also shared the same birthday (not just the day, but also the year). Two fellows with all of that strangely in common sitting surfside half the world away having a beer. Strange enough, I remember thinking. Just one of those things. But later that evening, when Louise and I returned for dancing with a few of our new-found friends in tow, he was back again.

Everybody was high, drinking and dancing like madmen—it felt so good, ripping loose like that on the sandy dance floor—the music loud and hypnotic, a big crowd of people all around the cabana and down the beach. In the midst of this throng I found myself talking with this guy again—Dave was his name—and we got into some brief, meaningless conversation, two guys from far away comparing observations, when suddenly the conversation turned serious.

"It's sure strange, you know?" I said. "To be here so far from home. To meet up with someone with the same name, born on the exact same day."

"Maybe it's not strange at all," he said, a little mischievously, like he was playing me.

"Why is that?" I asked.

And his eyes briefly flashed blue and maniacal—truly it happened like this, as though lightning flickered behind his veiled facade: "Because I'm the Devil," he said. And for an instant, I had to consider that it might be true. Satan stood there grinning at me as I pondered this seriously for one awkward moment. A brief, almost indiscernible pulse of paranoia rippled through me (what did I say about signs? about paying attention?).

But it was all too crazy of course. Perhaps I had read too much Dostoyevsky in college, had peered over the edge one too many times on my regular journeys to the precipice. At any rate I was just out there far enough—both mentally and physically—to consider any possibility. For one surreal second I pondered something that seemed to rip a small hole in the fabric of the longest-running dream I have ever known. But I have heard the music, heard enough of the music of the world in all its disguises and subtleties, taking me out as it has so many times to the spaces where all is broken down in dazzling and blissful dissolution, to know that the music will always bring you home again, make everything whole.

If you get confused, just listen to the music play...

I stepped away, saw my beautiful wife of about five days twirling and hopping to the heavy beat by herself amid the revelers. Then I smiled and waved the Devil off with my hand, gave him a look that said his con was up, he'd gotten the wrong guy. "Get outta here," I said. And I hit the dance floor.

It was probably only a day or two later that I lost my wedding ring. Louise had picked out our bands. They were simple and very fine, white gold with a little border design and inside bearing the inscription of our wedding day. Our rings didn't have much of a history. Mine is gone. Hers is somewhere safe, hidden away. She died wearing it, along with the diamond engagement ring I had given her. The man from the funeral home gave them to me as though they were the keys to a wrecked car.

Until Louise slipped it on my finger at our wedding, I had never worn a ring before. The fit was a little loose. I still don't know what happened to it, when exactly it went missing—it could have happened anytime. We were out there swimming in soft, hypnotic waters, running fingers through the sand, rubbing lotions into skin. It was just gone one day, in the middle of our honeymoon. It might still be drifting among the shells and currents along the ocean floor. It may have fallen behind a pillow or been lost on the beach. Someone could have picked it up, read the inscription inside, and wondered.

Of course, as a watcher for signs, I saw immediately that losing my wedding ring could be a foreboding. But even if you're the kind who heeds omens (I don't: I only watch for them), that first, faint intuition that you're in the crosshairs of impending menace is easily dismissed. I earned myself a little grief for losing my ring: that is to be expected. But then Louise shrugged it off. We would get a new one. It was only money, after all. We were on our honeymoon. We quickly forgot about it.

Still, in light of all that came after, it leads to a haunting question. If that ring was a symbol of our marriage, and I lost the ring... Is that where the trouble started? No. Was it something intentional on my part, some unconscious throwing off of my commitment? No. It's preposterous. Was the Devil present? No. He was just some drifter construction worker from Iowa.

But these things are working on me still. What *of* fate? There is evil in the world. You can choose to ignore it, but it might find you anyway. You can go after it—try to take it down—but it will drive you mad. You can hide from it, hold tight to the one you love, but it might come and take her anyway.

Omens and visitations of evil. Chance or fate? Where do these bad things begin? You'll believe almost anything, just to have some reason. You will blame yourself before allowing for an empty, Godless universe. And just how in hell does that work? The way it invades your life, steals off with your sweetheart, beats you for dead like a dirty dog, and then leaves you feeling responsible somehow. What

kind of sadistic and cowardly race are we that call ourselves
the architects of our own pain?

Maybe it *was* all my fault. If not mine, then whose? Bad
things were happening and I was the only one who was
always there. Louise was there for some, had suffered the
most, but after she was gone it was all on me. It kept
coming.

Maybe it would be better if I could say goodbye, but I
can't. I've got to keep missing her, even if it makes it harder.
And some days it does seem to be getting harder. It's not
the managing of things. I manage fine. And we are not
alone. Plenty of people are looking out for Robin and me.
Still I find myself lonely for Louise. She's my wife. I'm her
husband—that is who I am.

I dream of her, and though I know in my dream that she's
dead I am almost able to convince myself otherwise, that
none of it happened and the dream is real (one time it *was*
real—I swear, she was there—I do know the difference by
now). When I wake up there is an immediate regret which
quickly passes. It doesn't even upset me anymore. I'm just
glad to have a little visit from her. I'll take what I can get.

I just want to talk to her. She was the one person I could
talk to about anything, so natural that of course I took it for
granted. There are levels of intimacy and we had
penetrated quite a few. That is a rare thing. It does not
happen with just anyone, and it takes time even when you
do find the one—at least it did for us. When love really
takes root, as ours finally did, you are not aware how thick
and tangled those roots grow below the ground, how deep
into they earth they set hold. And when it is uprooted there
is the strangest feeling of exposure, as if nothing is holding

you down and you could be carried off anywhere. Tumbleweed.

I see elderly people with much more compassion now. I had never known loneliness before. It must be so awful to live a long time and watch as all the people you have ever known continue to fall away. Finally there is only you. You're sitting in some nursing home actually looking forward to being dead. Everyone you know is already there. A big party going on in a place you're too tired to even wonder about and you're stuck there by yourself in a dark room wearing a diaper.

And there's a difference between loneliness and being alone. When I was younger, more foolish, I had raised the status of aloneness to that of a sacred art. Finding that singular space of yours, not touching anyone else, not having to rely on anyone for anything, or at least convincing yourself that you don't need a soul. I now can pass it off as a youthful pose, arrogance, stupidity—and fortunately whatever cool self-sufficiency I possessed existed solely in my mind. I made friends in spite of myself, thankfully, while there was still time.

It is good, I guess, to set yourself apart a little, while you are still young. While you're so casually ignoring all the advantages of birth and upbringing that put you in a position to pronounce yourself an American original, perhaps all you are really doing is giving yourself a little room to formulate your plan. Fifteen years ago, the time I'm talking about—those heady, brooding, hard-drinking college years. Finding people like yourself, talking it all through, covering everything—literally the meaning of it all. Amazing how as you get older your life kind of comes with you, like a story. You can examine it that way, revise your take on things, grow a little.

Maybe you can use the past. Maybe that way it can't use you. Or maybe it's there to haunt you with the echoes, make you re-live things again and again as though it wasn't hard enough the first time. All I know is that something is working on me, something I didn't ask for, and I'm never going to be able to forget. It's all part of the story now. I've got to accommodate.

Life and the way it teases you. I can see the advantages when it giveth, but I start to wonder when it taketh away. That's pure, blind faith, what it's asking for. That's puzzle enough to hold off sleep, keep your eye on the glare of the moon in your window.

To deal with it well you're supposed to make yourself hard, which is cowardly. We're here to feel, I guess. Let it run over you, let it float you back up. It's not necessarily good or bad—it's just bigger than you. Maybe to proceed beyond suffering you have to suffer. I'm colossally fucked up and confused by this, as I am by all learning experiences. This is a learning experience, isn't it? I would like to know at least that much. As long as I know that Louise is going to be alright, I'll step to the front of the class. I'll endure anything if I know that I haven't actually lost her. Is that so insolent? Taken that way my blasphemy is really a backhanded compliment. If God created her, is it wrong to rage when He takes her away?

Our trip to Florida was pleasant. Sunshine on the soul is always good. Secretly I longed for a miracle, though it never took place. Time may heal me, but it moves the same in sunshine and waves—that is, slowly.

There were the three children, my mother and father, my brother and his wife, and me. The last time I had been down there Louise had come and Robin was just a baby. I kept remembering that trip and felt awkward, like a fifth wheel, and the sights and sounds called up memories. I missed her around every corner, under certain shady trees. The kids kept us all moving. I had exactly thirty minutes to myself for the week, driving off on an errand to get ice cream, and I took a detour down a dead-end road to where the suburban sprawl met up with the flat, ancient, green country. There was a little glade there, at the end of the road where it circled around and headed back from where it came. For some reason I half-expected to see Louise there. When she did not appear I suddenly wished to stop the car and weep. The ice cream was melting. I turned around and drove back.

I was able to get away for golf a few times, with my father and brother, but mostly we entertained the kids, took them to museums, aquariums, swam in the pool. Robin and I liked the beach best of all. The Gulf of Mexico was not far away, and ever since she was a baby Robin has loved to play in the sand and surf. She is happiest when her play is free form, random, pure expression, and the energy of the seashore seems to absorb everything she can give it—it entrances her completely and she seems to step right in, chameleon-like. Her eyes are blue like the water, her hair fine and blond like the sand. Her skin is milky white, like seashells, like her mother's. She's an imaginative child, has some powerful inner life, and she goes deeper inside at the beach as if hypnotized by the light off the water, the rush and music of the breakers feeling up the shore.

I tried to get her to walk with me to hunt for seashells, but she wouldn't come, and she didn't even play much with her cousins. It was a joyous, solitary dance she was performing, and I finally was content to sit on a blanket and watch her dart in and out of the waves along the water's edge. Robin has a strong little body, buoyant and springy. As she ran out into the surf I noticed that in mid-stride her feet were both off the ground—so light, flying almost. She sang and talked to herself, tittered out into the frothy foam of the sea, rolled herself in the white sand like a powdered cookie, chased gulls off our little area of beach like a border collie—rushing them up with willful intent, leaping into them with her arms outstretched, like she wanted to take off with them.

I envied her, and I was able to relax finally, vicariously. All of life should be so spontaneous and free. She was like an artist, so completely absorbed that her play and her work had become one. The sand and wind and water were her media, the sun was her light—and her mother, who so loved to sit on a sandy beach beside the sea, was inside her, dreaming.

15

Now back again in the dormant North. Winter into spring: subtle and hopeful. A soft, four-inch snow fell overnight, but by mid-morning the air was warm and the sky delicate, yellow, promising. This morning, out walking the dog, I heard a cardinal singing his melodious, distinctive song. Singing like he meant it, like he was happy. He can feel it in his very wingtips, the change coming. I saw him high up in the black branches, a splash of red against the pillowing sky, the snow breaking off the branches like sugar cubes, sifting down through the trees on the urging of a southerly breeze.

I've been looking out my window, studying the winter, looking for signs. We're definitely on the upswing now, riding the rising arc of the sun. We're beyond that spot—that spot in the cold hollow of winter—where you're just tired and hopeless and stuck dead in the middle of it. Where you wouldn't want to go back even if you could, and you need some kind of encouragement to even move forward anymore, spring seeming so far off and idyllic that heaven is more likely.

It was in that hollow of deepest winter, just a few years ago, that Louise had her bone marrow transplant in a big, inner-city hospital nearby. When they found the cancer had spread to her lung, her doctors were quick to offer us the new hope that a transplant might work. We were just as quick to believe it *could* work: it had to. The surgery had obviously not gotten all of the tumor. There had been chemotherapy and radiation. Now we were on to Plan D, or was it Plan G or J? Whatever the case, we were running out of letters of the alphabet, we knew.

Of course she needed the referrals, the usual paperwork and authorization from the insurance company, which would be reluctant to cover her because the procedure is expensive and Louise was becoming—though nobody would actually say it—a hopeless case. There was a whole new team of doctors and a new hospital to deal with, which was kind of intimidating at first, and because they were new every test and appointment was accomplished only after we had negotiated a whole new minefield of paperwork. I can see poor Louise on the telephone, in her desperation arranging for this test and that appointment, trying to keep her composure and patience as the tangled bureaucratic vines grew thicker about her rapidly fraying nerves. We really needed a full-time secretary to simply administer her medical treatments. It is tiresome to even think back on. The frustration is more than even a healthy person can handle, much less a woman who sees her life slowly unraveling even as her active toddler is wrapped about her knees.

And it just goes around and around forever, faxes, records, x-rays, insurance documents—a cyclone of paper that seems to pick up steam as it churns across the medical prairie. Suffice it to say that the hospital still has not been entirely paid up for Louise's care, still sends me bills to this day. I of course refer them to my insurance company—and the insurance company, depending on the day of the week and how smoothly their bureaucracy is humming along, either pays up or suddenly loses all record that we ever existed.

Whatever. Throughout these four-plus years I have refused—for the most part successfully—to get caught up in the labyrinthine saga of paperwork regarding Louise's medical care. Several majestic trees have given their lives for the bills that have arrived in my mailbox, only to be tossed directly in the trash. In the midst of all our more immediate, daily problems, I would have been a mad fool to give these matters a single thought. Occasionally, well-meaning people would ask how we were handling the mounting medical costs. I think I surprised them with my ignorance of the whole matter. "If I ever tried to figure out the hassles with the insurance company and the medical bills," I told them, "it would be all I do."

That was one problem I dutifully ignored, and I would not let Louise worry about it for an instant. She was going to get the best care and *somebody* would pay for it, someday. Even the remotest chance was worth every penny. I was ready to give up all we had—and still would—to get her back. At the appointed time, on the appointed day, they could leave Robin and me standing naked and penniless in the street if we knew that Louise would drop from the sky there. The rest would be easy. It would be fun building it all back up.

The bills still come, although they have slowed to a trickle. I'm pestered now by one final, very determined collection agency that calls and asks for Louise. They represent the hospital where she had her transplant, but they haven't yet figured out that Louise died more than two years ago. I pick up the phone and immediately know who it is—some resolute Pekinese of a woman calling from her kennel somewhere in Kentucky: "If y'all don't send me a check for seventeen thousand dollars we *will* take court action to collect on this debt!"

I just hang up the phone. Fuck them. I'm not paying. That's why I have insurance.

Stem cell transplant is the term for it, actually, and despite their continual perfecting of the process, despite the best mood-altering and painkilling drugs they can administer, it is still a brutal procedure that can only be justified by the sheer desperation of the patient who must endure it. And before she could even qualify Louise had to undergo a whole series of painful tests and hospitalizations, any of which, depending on what it determined, could possibly jeopardize her eligibility to receive the treatment at all.

First they needed to check her bone marrow, make sure it was clean, free of cancer. So they dug into her hip with a long, fat, shovel-nosed needle—no anesthesia—and shaved off a piece of bone. Then they wanted to biopsy the growth in her lung—although they were very sure it was cancerous, they had to be certain. They stuck another long needle through her back, between a couple of ribs, pierced her lung and probed for a tissue sample with the aid of CAT Scan imagery. For this also she had to be fully conscious and without general anesthesia, in case the lung were to collapse—which, in this case, it did, and for a brief moment she was in danger of dying on the table. She was hospitalized for a week, and during that stay she caught a nasty infection that also nearly killed her. They allowed her to come home, but for the next two weeks she was forced to carry around an IV bag with the most powerful antibiotic known to the world strapped to her hip.

Then there was another hospital stay, for more chemotherapy: I honestly forget what for. Finally she spent a couple of days hooked up to a machine, kind of like dialysis, while they harvested stem cells from her blood. The stem cells, we were told, act as the building blocks—the foundation cells—for the blood, for every kind of tissue and organ in the body. These were collected in a plastic bag, sealed up, and stuck in the freezer.

She would need those blood cells later, because the chemotherapy they were going to give her this time made all the potions she had received up to that point seem like Kool-Aid. These chemicals would blast away everything in her body that wasn't nailed to her skeleton—hopefully the cancer, too. The chemicals would be so toxic they would *kill* her for all practical purposes, destroy her immune system to where it couldn't build itself back up again—except they now had those healthy stem cells on ice, waiting. The idea was to bombard her system with lethal chemicals, lay *everything* flat—and then, just before she died of an overdose of poison (if all went according to plan), they would send those healthy stem cells back in—transplant them—and they would save her.

We had a big problem in figuring out how we were going to care for Louise and Robin in two different places at the same time. I was still working—or at least going through the motions—and at the time we were sending Robin to a rather institutional daycare near home. It was not a terrible place, but it was not great—songs and games, paints and puzzles, dozens of snot-nosed kids firing toys at each others' heads as bored teenage girls looked on. I felt horrible leaving Robin there every morning, felt like I was dumping her there, but we had no choice. For the transplant and the aftercare, Louise was going to have to stay in the hospital for three weeks, and even after that she would not come directly home but would instead stay at her mother's house, where it was quiet and clean and she could rest completely for a few weeks more.

When she did come home it would be how long—who knew?—before she would be up to caring for a daughter who knew nothing of what was happening, who would demand all of her mother that any two-year-old would. Though I was feeling fortunate to have so many people available to help—there was Louise's mother, my parents and family, plenty of friends—I also knew that I would be stretched between Robin, Louise, and work, and that I would not be able to give any of them enough attention. It would be hard just keeping everyone covered, and when I was able to stop obsessing over how we could pull it off the real concern began flooding in, and I allowed myself to be simply frightened for Louise, for myself and Robin— all of us. This was more than likely our last chance. Christmas came and went as we approached the transplant with a mixture of dread and whatever hope we could scrape together.

And we did have hope. We had to try. The building was burning and Louise had kept climbing to the top floor. She was trying so hard. I felt I was right there with her, flames reaching up around our feet, and it was a long way to the ground. The transplant was like a big pillow laid out for us far, far below. Aim for the big red dot, hold hands, and close your eyes. We had to make the jump.

.

As if high-dose chemotherapy were not terrible enough, it also isolates the patient. During her transplant procedure and for several weeks after, Louise would have to live in a sterilized environment, because her immune system would be totally blown away. Any simple bacteria or virus could enter her system, make her terribly sick or even kill her. This meant that for several weeks she would not have the comfort of Robin—could not even see her, much less hold her—because children especially are incubators of all kinds of germs. The fewer people around the better, but she would need *somebody* around the clock because she was going to be in rough shape. We decided that her mother would stay with Louise, I would work during the day and take care of Robin in the evenings, and my mother and sisters would help out when somebody needed a break.

Late in January one day, they started. The brightness of the room, the efficiency and compassion of the nurses, the technology—all belied the awfulness of the chemicals, the desperation of what was happening and the waning hope that it could work. There would be four days of high-dose chemotherapy, four different poisons dripping in each day, the last one the most awful (some hooded executioner without a name, or a name that I've forgotten). Thankfully over time they've perfected to some degree the sedation they can give you. Louise was pumped up with mood-enhancers, pain medicines, antidepressants—drugs with names that sounded like bad poetry but were able, at least momentarily, to mercifully trick her brain into a state of emotional tolerance.

They dripped in the first bag. She slept through it, mostly. She seemed fine that first day, and we even had a few laughs that evening. Maybe this wouldn't be so bad. Her mother was with her during the morning hours. My office was nearby and I was able to come in on my way to and from work. In the evening I picked up Robin and took her home for the night. Robin would ask where her mother was, but by that time she had become used to Louise being away for a few days or even a week at a time.

By the end of the second day and another treatment Louise began to pale—her face was ashen gray, her lips thin and blue. She looked cold. Still, the drugs seemed to be holding off much of the discomfort. Her eyes were merry as the stars. She joked with the nurses as she had always done. She had probably been hospitalized a dozen times by this point, and without fail the nurses seemed to take a special liking to Louise—they took extra care with her, I could tell, because they could see she was brave. Perhaps they identified with her. Most of them were women of about the same age. With few exceptions I was utterly amazed at their ability to combine compassion and competence—the way they balanced those two qualities, knowing that one was no good without the other. The energy and enthusiasm they brought to such a difficult profession—I have no idea how they pulled it off, day after day. The best nurses could breeze in and out of the room in thirty seconds and somehow leave us all feeling more hopeful, as though with such people on our side there was no way we could lose.

The third day another bag, a different chemical. She was a little more alert, having some pain, but still dreamy, though she couldn't eat or drink anything. She slept a lot, but it was a writhing half-sleep, and it was clear that the mood-enhancing drugs were losing their tug-of-war with the poisonous, hard-core chemicals. She slept fitfully, half-conscious that she was almost through it, until finally we arrived at the fourth day— the awful day—the one they had been gently warning us about because the chemical was so toxic.

Things to this point, though not pleasant, had seemed at least tolerable, not as awful as we had feared, though Louise was certainly feeling terrible even under massive sedation. I stopped at the hospital again that morning on my way down to work. When I left I felt the familiar tug of guilt, but her mother was with her and there was nothing I could do.

I went to work, and from there I had to go home early to rescue Robin from her daycare for some reason. I brought her home in the late afternoon and immediately there was a call from the hospital—a nurse calling from Louise's bedside—saying it might be a good idea (an urgency in her voice) if I came down to the hospital soon. Then Louise got on the phone briefly and asked could I please come quickly, her voice dripping with a strange tone of desperation I had never heard before. Immediately I felt awful for having not been there, for having allowed myself the luxury of secretly hoping she would slide through that last day uneventfully. My sister had been on call for backup, and she packed a bag for overnight and came to the house to watch Robin.

When I got to the hospital I was astonished and sickened to see the look on Louise's face, the transformation that had taken place since I had seen her in the morning. The last chemical had certainly done its job. She looked as though she had gone fifteen rounds with the heavyweight champion. Her cheeks were badly swollen, her skin seemingly on fire, searing red flesh almost exploding from her face. In her eyes, when she saw me, there was an instant of relief, as though she had built it up in her mind that when I got there everything was going to be alright.

But then quickly came the realization that it was just me, that I brought no magic with me, and she just gave in and let the agony overtake her. She tried to speak. Her voice was metallic and desperate, remote, otherworldly. I suddenly felt as limp and useless as a rag doll, but at least a doll she could hold. I climbed through all her tubes and wires and monitors and lay beside her as she writhed and twisted in her tiny hospital bed.

In breathless half-phrases she described her pain, how it seemed so elusive, seemed to be everywhere at once—in her back, her head, now shooting down her legs. I have never seen such desperation in a person, such panic in the search for a way out: I'm sure that at that moment, if someone had handed her a loaded gun, she would have gratefully put the barrel in her mouth and fired. I felt horribly inadequate, couldn't touch her, couldn't reach the pain.

I hounded the nurses for some kind of solution. Finally they were able to reach her doctor and he prescribed some morphine. Around three in the morning the narcotic began to take hold and Louise began to relax, even smiling a little as she allowed herself a moment of triumph for having completed this leg of the marathon at least. She began to get drowsy, and as I lay beside her I whispered in her ear that it was all over now—at least the hardest part was over—the poison had done its grim work and tomorrow was the first day of her comeback, her resurrection. She smiled at this and yawned. "Thanks, honey," she said. "Now could you please get the hell out of my bed?"

And as I climbed out through the tubes and wires I really did feel hopeful that she had finally crossed over to safety. Nothing, I encouraged myself, not even the most rabid tumor, could survive that kind of punishment. I even felt an odd sense of security that night, half-sleeping on a chair in the corner of her room, all the monitors and machines humming away, the nurses calmly, deftly slipping in and out every few minutes in their bright scrubs and silent sneakers. All this medicine and science, all these brilliant, dedicated people—surely they would help us find the way through. Surely they could save her.

I staggered home the following morning to find that the furnace had broken down the night before. It had been brutally cold overnight and the thermostat inside registered forty-two degrees. My sister had not wanted to trouble me. She had piled five or six blankets on top of Robin and had herself slept in all her clothes and a winter coat. She had looked for more blankets but, finding none, instead curled up under a couple tablecloths she found in the linen closet. We could see our breath in the kitchen as we spoke. But there was a pot of hot coffee going when I came in, and the whole thing seemed so ridiculous I could only laugh with her.

I fished out the yellow pages and opened it up to Heating & Cooling. I thought now this. I thought terrific, coldest morning of the winter and I'm going to need emergency repairs on my furnace. This isn't going to cost much. There are probably dozens of guys who will do it for free.

It's difficult to tell so much of this. I hope it proves to help somehow. I'm trying to get rid of it. If you expect it to fly, you've got to give it wings. You're supposed to learn from experience, and I *am* learning. But it seems the smarter I get the more it hurts. As a friend once said, I'd rather be dumb and happy.

I wonder when I'm going to reach that much-publicized "acceptance" stage—I find myself resisting it. I want to hold onto my bitterness a little longer. Bitterness is tangible. I'm skeptical of acceptance. It's built up as a kind of peace, but it seems to me a lot like death—lying down and letting things just happen as they will. Why would I want to feel something like death? That's what death is for.

No, acceptance is a bill of goods. The more accepting I become the more ridiculous it seems. If acceptance is about renouncing your desires, then why do I desire things at all? I like my desires—they define me. I want, therefore I am. I wanted Louise, got her, lost her—didn't like it. And I don't like the idea of giving anything else up.

I don't think we're supposed to escape that cycle of love and loss. I think it is entirely the point. I'll complain as loudly as anyone about it, but there it is. Maybe, as souls, we're all out here experiencing different things, living out our preconceived destinies, colliding with each other and bouncing off each other like molecules, some of us experiencing joy and prosperity, others loneliness, others pain, it having been our choice or God's choice—maybe nobody's choice: just chance and the Grand Experiment. We're supposed to go about our business, care or not care for whatever we choose, have our experiences however bad or sensational. And then later, when it's all over, we can look back and see what we've learned.

So go ahead and embrace your desires. It is the most honest way. Go ahead and love things that you know you will ultimately lose. It is all impermanent anyway. Only do not accept anything. Do not lie down. The dead can accept things for us. They have more than enough time.

A couple of days after the last of the poison was dripped in, Louise was moved to an apartment building adjacent to the hospital. All the transplant patients were put up there and then shuttled by bus to the clinic at the hospital each day. The apartment building was bland and somewhat dim, but comfortable. Louise and her mother spent most of each day at the hospital for her follow-up care, then returned in the evening to the apartment.

On the day of the transplant—her "new birthday" as Louise called it—I sat with Louise and held her hand as the nurse and doctor checked and double-checked the serial numbers on the IV bags of stem cells they pulled from a small cooler filled with dry ice. For all the expense of this state-of-the-art procedure, it happened very quickly. Louise sat on a bed in a tiny room. They gave her a mint candy to suck on, a bed pan to vomit into, and hooked up the bag of now-defrosted stem cells to her IV tube. Almost immediately her face went a deep red as the cold fluid raced into her bloodstream. Then she swooned, nearly fainted, and threw up.

The room suddenly smelled of rotten tomato juice, and the doctor explained that this was the chemical used to preserve the stem cells, that Louise was actually tasting this preservative as it coursed through her veins. They pumped in three more bags this way, and the whole thing took less than an hour. Louise looked tired and pale, felt awful, but she smiled and joked the whole time and allowed herself the hope that it would all be worth it.

She stayed in the apartment for a few weeks after that, slowly getting stronger, though certainly now she was very pale and thin—taking on the trademark look of the emaciated cancer patient that we hoped was only a low point in her return to the beauty she had always been. Finally she received permission to go home—home to her mother's house where she could rest quietly. She was still quite ill and her immune system was very weak, but the transplant had been a success at least in the fact that the transplanted cells had "taken" and were now multiplying and growing inside her. It was still to soon to tell whether the chemotherapy had done its job, whether it had eliminated or at least arrested the growth of the one large and several smaller tumors that had grabbed hold in her lungs. After such an ordeal it would be too overwhelming to even consider that it may have all been in vain. For now we only wanted her home.

During these long, grim winter days a subtle change had occurred in our house. Robin now looked to me as the one who took care of her. She had grown accustomed to her mother not being around, though she asked questions and wondered where Louise was and when she could see her. Still she was very young, concerned mostly with her immediate world, and she was a normal, happy child. So the excitement was greater for me and Louise when the doctors gave us the okay to bring Robin down to see her mother for the first time in nearly a month.

I put Robin in a new dress, told her we were going to see somebody really special, that it was a surprise. Louise of course had been waiting weeks for that morning to arrive, and when Robin walked in, when the two of them saw each other and Robin—suddenly remembering this familiar if somewhat distorted face—ran into her mother's arms, I stepped back into a little hallway and cried a little. Louise still looked awful—she moved around slowly, stiff and hunched forward—but she laughed weakly and clung to Robin, following her around the room as Robin happily explored this strange place, reaching for her when she could catch up to her as though Robin was an apparition, something not quite real. And it must have been almost unbelievable after what she had been through—this the latest, most intense battle in what was becoming a darkening war—to suddenly see her only child having grown a month in her absence. She must have felt like a distance had been established between them, that she would have to struggle to make up for that time, like she was falling behind, falling away.

A few weeks later, when she came back to our own house on a cold, bright Sunday afternoon, there was for me a sweetness and a pain, a sense that for good or ill she had had enough and I was not going to let them have her anymore. She was ours and she was home, whole or not, cured or—probably not. I just wanted her home, hour by hour, day by day, for as long as we could have her.

We had her and she was still ours. We would hold her for as long as we could. It was starting to look like that would not be long.

16

As I read over what I've written so far I see where my obvious inclination toward the melancholy leaves an impression that my life as a single father has been one long, uninterrupted frustration. The truth is that I'm as proud and happy as any father could be—though at times I wonder if it is a case of having too much of a good thing.

Robin brings a lot of herself to the party and then keeps coming. She completely overwhelms me. I find myself *managing* her more than actually raising her—I am a man, after all. I operate more on the edges of her life, secure the perimeter, and I think I'm pretty good at it. But of course she needs more. Had Louise lived I'm sure the division of labor would have found me doing much of what I'm doing now, more of the cooking and cleaning, paying bills, running the household, planning the college fund—paving the way. Louise would have spent more time engaging Robin at eye level, reading stories, dressing up dolls, painting pictures, going on nature walks and collecting bugs in a jar. Louise was like a big kid anyway, and I am too insular to be of any real use to an imaginative five-year-old.

Probably not without a few arguments along the way, we would have divided up the responsibilities and settled into our roles as mother and father to Robin.

But with things as they are I'm scrambling just to keep up. It is so much work to raise even one child, and in trying to be both mother and father I find myself making compromises, restrained by time and the limits of my sanity into simply being as real as I can possibly be for Robin. I give her as much as I've got on any given day, and I try not to beat myself up over what she's missing.

Robin would prefer to see me as a giant playmate, would lead me around by the hand from morning until night if I let her. But I'm restrained by the fact that there is always—always—something that needs to be done around the house. I can never catch up to the housework, much less squeeze in a day's work in the middle. I kid myself that I could handle single parenthood beautifully if I didn't have to work at all, but in reality a day at work is much easier than chasing a five-year-old girl through her labyrinth for fourteen hours. By contrast work is easy. The office is a quiet, beautiful place—and far away.

On most days my physical presence will have to be enough—me doing my thing, Robin doing hers, and at least we're together. Of course she fights for my attention, and of course I give her what I can, but I have to create some space for myself or Robin will devour me. She is persistent, demands a platform, at times annoys me to a fury, but I wouldn't have it any other way.

It is a grudging, respectful truce we've arrived at, one that is not always pretty to witness. She knows I love her and she exploits that. When I've had enough I have to let her know, often with force, or the message does not get through. After our little battles we always make up. We both acknowledge our share of the blame, both apologize. Sometimes we go at it right up until bedtime—I literally have to wrestle her into bed. She cries and calls for me as I simmer in my chair. Burnt and tired. Nothing left for today. No more. It's just a ploy, I tell myself. She's just working you. "Go to *sleep!*" I holler. Then finally the house is quiet and I feel terrible. I go in and lie down next to her, brush the hair from her face, watch her chest rising and falling.

We have fun together too. On weeknights we will go to the library or, in nice weather, ride our bicycles to the Frosty Freeze for ice cream. I take her to ballet classes and art lessons. On weekends we visit museums or the zoo, go to the movies. My family is still close and at least monthly we seem to reassemble like Parliament at somebody's house, where Robin and all her little cousins can run around for hours.

Like any little girl Robin has a bottomless capacity for play, and like any man in his thirties I have a limited tolerance for the minutiae of a little girl's world. I look forward to the years ahead, when we can do more things that we both enjoy. I hope she takes to sports—we can find plenty in common there. I'll coach and help her practice. I want to take her hiking and camping—I'm a novice myself, but we can learn together. We can get dressed up for plays and concerts, even travel a little—all when she's a little older. Right now Robin's world is necessarily tedious. I have trouble getting down on the floor to dress up Barbie dolls. I don't like cutting and pasting little pieces of construction paper. I still can't wrap Christmas gifts or decorate cookies. My attention span for craftwork is as short and blunt as my fingers—I'm waiting for activities that involve arms and legs, or the mind. There has to be something in it for me or I grow impatient. I just need a little more space, a little more time. Miles and distance, open air, expanding ourselves out into the world. We're getting there. When we do, I hope she's still speaking to me.

I realize that I'll miss these days when they're gone, but at her age of five, while Robin is learning by trial and error, by scrutinizing and experimenting, I find myself tapping my foot impatiently, trying to keep things moving along, always rushing the schedule—perhaps trying to push us both into that golden future when things will supposedly get a little easier. Parenting a small child is, literally, micromanaging—not exactly my specialty. At times it seems I move Robin through her day like a chess piece—out of bed and to the breakfast table, into the car and off to school, back home again, toward the bathtub and into her pajamas, brush your teeth and now, finally, breathlessly, into bed where always—every day—we wind up with at least a half hour of storytime before she drifts off grudgingly to sleep.

Our day begins at seven in the morning and ends at nine in the evening—a fourteen-hour day and I can say in all honesty that I'm working for the family business the entire time. Fourteen hours, seven days a week, my lone reprieve each day coming only after Robin is asleep and I collapse into the sheltering arms of my favorite chair before the numbing television, remote control in hand. And give us this day our daily beer or three.

As much as I love Robin and as much time and effort I put into caring for her, I have no idea how well I'm actually doing. Who is she, really? And how much of that has to do with me? Of course she is, first and always, *herself*. I can only guide her so much—my influence goes so far and then the line is blurred where nature and circumstance join in. I'm convinced that children are born with their personalities already intact. As Robin's father I can only help her weed out her lesser qualities, turn her better side toward the sun. This is delicate work that requires wisdom and restraint—not to suggest that I have either of these, but at least I know I'm aiming for.

Robin charges ahead, and I pull her back. She resists and I push her along. We clash constantly. But what is good for me is not always best for Robin. I want to protect her, to keep her from falling. But if I don't let her go she'll miss out on things and resent me for it, or become timid. I want to teach her good manners, but not to the point that I squeeze all the spontaneity and joy out of her, to where she's afraid to move for fear of giving offense to some social code she could not possibly understand. I want to pay attention to her, but not to where she thinks I'm her personal plaything without a life of my own. We're slowly learning to live with one another, but there are always eruptions of anger and tears. Robin already is showing signs of a strong will, and lately I'm just crankier than hell. The atmosphere is ripe in our house. Hurricanes occasionally do form and have doubtless drifted across the emerald lawns and crashed ashore in the living rooms of our neighbors from time to time.

I'm raising Robin by feel, mostly. I try to do what comes naturally, give her some room. I don't believe in sitting on her anymore than I would sit on anyone else. My basic approach, if I even have one, is to let Robin be as free and expressive as I can possibly stand. This may be harder for me now but will be better for her when she's grown. I let her run. When she goes too far, I pull her back in, but at least she is getting her legs beneath her.

I don't want to be her pal, either. I'm her father. I don't hold the stone tablets or anything, but I'm smarter than her. Robin is a little person, I'm a big person, and we live in the same house. I'm in charge, no question, but there is some give and take. She is strong-willed, likes to get her way. Sometimes I let her, other times not. That's what life is like, and she may as well find out now about limitations, discover where her will ends and someone else's begins.

So she leans and I lean back. It can be tiresome. She negotiates *everything*. "Daddy," she'll say, "how about if I eat *five* of my green beans and then we go for ice cream? Deal?" And I'll say, "How about you eat them all or no television tomorrow?" Then she counters and I give a little, back and forth we go, sometimes with tears, incredible theatrics and high drama. She runs through the whole gamut before she'll give in. Eventually, she eats her beans.

I was not completely unprepared for all of this. Robin is like her mother. I've seen these tricks before. Their temperaments are so similar. Louise carried around a few embers from the ancestral Celtic fire. When I see that same tempestuousness in Robin, and despite the fact that it makes my job more difficult, I cherish it, even nurture it. That is literally fruit from the original tree.

I jokingly refer to her as the Queen, but Robin has carried a certain regal intensity since the day she was born. As an infant her aspect was more sober—we thought we had given birth to the reincarnation of Cotton Mather. Her gaze was level, penetrating, striking out like a laser from her deep-set, icy blue eyes at whatever she pleased. When she trained those eyes on you it almost made you feel small. I honestly think she hurt my mother's feelings on occasion with her apparent disregard.

And while now she is blossoming into a friendly, uninhibited, at times very silly little girl, she maintains a sturdy sense of herself—not disdainful, but sure. She is charming and she knows it. I encourage that sassiness to a point. Perhaps I'm creating a monster. "You're awfully smart," I'll tell her, "for such a pretty girl." And she'll reply forthrightly: "Yes. I *know* I am."

To be beautiful and smart, those are the qualities I wish for Robin as she grows. I want her to know that she is both, and I want to set the idea in hard—now and often—because her confidence will come under fire when she's older. Brilliant and beautiful—that is the woman I hope she sees years from now when she looks in the mirror or, more importantly, looks within. Louise was both beautiful and smart. I love that in a woman, any woman. Why wouldn't I want that for Robin? A beautiful, intelligent woman can do anything she pleases.

17

Throughout her long illness, and especially as things turned decidedly worse throughout that last aching summer, Louise began to splash about in the waters (drowning, as she was) for some spiritual truths that she could grab hold of for comfort, if not for salvation or even a miracle. Only the few people on earth who have experienced such desperation and survived can possibly know the fear and loneliness she must have encountered as that mysterious, unforgiving black wall loomed ever nearer.

Louise had always been strong spiritually. She knew how to nourish her soul with art and music, observations of nature, though she had strayed from any kind of formal religion. In her illness people sent her things. People she hardly knew sent prayer books, books of affirmations and new age self-help philosophy, numerous bibles, cards with heartfelt, hand-written notes and little inspirational messages on them. Words: trying to bolster her up, and she appreciated it, read as much as she could in the hope that some message might act as the key, unlock some door in her

mind and release a torrent of archangels of mercy throughout her body—cleansing her. She was open to any idea,
would accept mercy from whichever direction it was offered.

Like many of our generation, she was quietly and in her
way a very religious person but without any singular creed.
We had both been raised Catholic, and she attended
Sunday mass through her college years before she stopped.
Louise was intellectual and open-minded and her feminism
would not allow for a Church that in all important matters
places women squarely one deferring step behind men. Her
problems were more with the institutional Church than the
faith, though the two for her were hard to distinguish and
consequently she backed away from both.

Our few arguments about religion centered around our
wedding ceremony and the question of baptism for Robin. I
was no better a Catholic than she was, probably worse, but I
didn't take my differences with the Church as personally as
she did, didn't react to it so viscerally. Typically, her reaction
to bringing religion into the most important events in our
lives was emotional and questioning. Why would we go
about the other 364 days of the year without religion and
then, on the most important day, invite it back in? And
typically my response would be non-confrontational and
diplomatic. I would answer that it was exactly those
occasions that needed some ritual to help them stand apart.
And back and forth. We checked one another: while she
was more honest and direct (to me, she was being silly and
overly dramatic), I was more circumspect (to her, I was fak-
ing, a hypocrite).

Those are among the few arguments I remember
winning. I wanted to be married in a Catholic church, by a
priest, and finally she agreed to it in the interest of the
feelings of family and of simply keeping doors open. If she

wasn't exactly thrilled to have a priest perform our wedding ceremony, I asked her to remember that it was not entirely about her, that there were people closely connected to us who had dreamed of this day since we were eating strained carrots from a jar, who saw it as a matter of great importance, of life and death: to be respectful of those people. I asked her to see that accommodating people's feelings didn't make you a hypocrite. She loathed hypocrisy, and this tack seemed to soften her. She allowed for the priest, and she asked her Unitarian minister to be co-celebrant. It turned out beautifully, though in meeting before the ceremony the two ministers eyed one another with a thinly veiled disdain. Later, when the time came, we also had Robin baptized in a Catholic church.

I didn't realize it at the time, but this little stand I had made—insisting on maintaining some tie to the religion we had both grown up with—was ultimately a good thing for Louise. Whether it "saved" her, well, who knows? I've got big problems with that concept. Everybody should be saved. If there is a God—if He is as big and powerful and forgiving as He says He is, and He's going around saving people—well, then I think He should save all of us. Religion should really not have anything to do with it. Regardless, and wherever Louise is now, I think her religion helped her in the end and I'm happy I helped her keep the door open.

As children we had both loved our religion. Louise's mother remains a church-going Christian. Her father was a Catholic and saw that she attended mass, though even he had his own ideas about things. I remember her telling how proud she had been of him, back when she was a grade-schooler, for sparing her the excruciating experience of the confessional on the grounds that he did not believe that children were capable of sin.

I grew up with a more intense Catholic experience than Louise—Catholic schools all the way through high school, mass every Sunday. I was even an altar boy for a few years, can still recall my mother rousing me out of bed at 5:30 one cold morning to serve my first mass. Our names had appeared in the church bulletin the Sunday before—mine and another boy's—but on that first morning the other boy failed to show and I had to do it all myself.

I was a wreck of nerves during the service, stumbling in my long red robe, fumbling with the crystal cruets like a dunce. And when I rang the bell during the Eucharistic Prayer I jangled the instrument so violently I drew a glare from Father Siegfried and nearly woke up one of the four sleeping people in attendance. Though the mass seemed to last an eternity, the well-fed friar actually raced through the entire service in less than fifteen minutes. He slowed his pace only momentarily after holy communion, when he rinsed his chalice with a full cruet of cheap table red and one infinitesimal drop of holy water—and then poured the blessed river down. After which I'm sure he returned to the rectory and slept until noon.

Going to church seemed as natural as breathing when I was a boy, and I loved it, never thought to question it. But as I got along into high school I think I just burned out, hit some quota of masses attended, and said enough. As teenagers my brother and I and our friends would get the keys to somebody's car and fulfill our Sunday obligation at St. Denny's or Our Lady of the Highway. Once I started college (now reading the great books, studying the philosophers, smoking grass with my friends in a dorm room and contemplating infinite space at three in the morning), much of organized religion began to seem ridiculous, even destructive. Still the truth at the center of it has always, for me, held up as something beautiful, as relevant as any other explanation for a mystery that has occupied people since we came down from the trees.

That beautiful part is still there, and that's enough for now. The people who go to church, who celebrate with the priest and one another, that's terrific for them. Those who need to go, go. Someday maybe I'll start going again. I love the mysticism of it, love the smells and the deep tones, the way the church is like an island, a hideout, outside of time almost. I think they started to lose me when they started trying to be hip, when they came at my generation with guitars and those silly songs, almost condescending the way they tried to reach us. But even that is unlikely—they were going to lose me anyway. Once out of the safe womb of childhood I began to see the world, in my strangely silent, confused adolescence, as a feast both beautiful and tragic at once. I became hell-bent for darker ideas. When I wanted to have a religious experience and listen to guitars, I discovered the Grateful Dead.

As July turned to August and the evenings grew cooler in the shade Louise talked about joining a church, but she still didn't want to go back to being a Catholic. In the final few months before she died she was in and out of the hospital more and more: a stay of three or four days, then a week, ten days. She almost preferred to be in the hospital rather than home. Dying is an intensely personal experience, and she liked the quiet of the hospital, the privacy. Though she hadn't broken any bonds with Robin, she had long since given up any idea of actively caring for her. She felt safer in the hospital, and the nurses all became her girlfriends, contrived to get her the nicest rooms, the private rooms. She had her television, her cards and letters. Mostly she had herself and thoughts long evaded, now catching her. So she thought them.

I was with her at the hospital one morning, the giving up coming on I could tell. All along she had only asked me to be her rock, and I tried to be that, though it's hard. You feel like a dumbass sometimes, just standing there, holding fast. You feel like you should be doing something. And then you realize you don't have the power to make this thing go away, that all you can do is try to absorb as much as possible, not let it move you, not let it sweep you away, be the one sure thing she can reach for and know you're going to be there, hard and fast and strong. Not moving—never.

She asked me again that day to be this for her. More true than our wedding vows, the way she asked, the way I took it. She said she felt like she was in a river, the water cold and rising, rushing up and over her, and I was the rock she was holding onto. She could feel her hand slipping: the water was too strong, but she was holding on, and could I be the rock for her? I said I could, but I was the saddest rock that ever was.

The parish we were part of—where Robin had been baptized—we had only been there for mass maybe once or twice. Nobody there knew us, or knew of Louise's trouble. It would be awkward, coming to them in our desperation, to ask for their help. I was starting to think of a funeral now. I didn't want it to be somebody who didn't know her saying the mass. I asked Louise if she wanted me to call a priest, to see if he might pay her a visit in the hospital. She was reluctant, but she agreed. I'm sure she was torn, her pride and her loathing of hypocrisy still strong. But she was probably thinking about a funeral, too. Of course she was.

I called the parish office and when I spoke to the priest

on the phone he sounded a little skeptical. Were we members of the parish? Was she near death? I told him she needed to talk to someone, that's all. Could he do that for us? He said he would try to get some time.

When I visited Louise in the hospital the next day, the priest was there, sitting in a chair next to her bed. He spoke very matter-of-factly about what was happening to her: she was dying, she was going to God, she was going to be alright. He asked us what kind of funeral we wanted. What kind of music should we have? Who would give her eulogy? Did she want to be buried or cremated? Did she want her funeral to be in the church at all? He was calm and smiling, made jokes. I couldn't believe we were having this conversation, acknowledging things this bluntly, when for so long we had defied this possibility: she was going to die.

It was such a relief, in a strange way. He stayed for only twenty minutes, but when he left Louise was shining, like a light had been turned on behind her eyes, her face flushed with color and smiling, and I could feel a little shift in the weight of the world, like maybe she was letting go, slipping away from the rock in the river, giving her permission to the water to take her home. I felt joy for her, could see something that looked like peace on her face for the first time in a while. Then I caught a look at my own face, in the mirror beside her bed, and I saw what I was going to be— this big, dumb rock, all alone in that river. I am still there.

Where I grew up I could hear the bells of St. Michael's church ring every hour. First came a kind of raucous chiming, a clarion of higher-pitched bells clanging as eagerly as a rooster on a summer's morning. Then, after a silent pause, came the low, somber tone of the big bell, deep and mournful, sounding once, twice, three times or more depending on the hour. Slow and steady, patiently sounding eight times for eight o'clock.

We could see the bell tower from our kitchen window. From our house we could walk down a narrow, wooded path and through to a large, green athletic field, across to church and school. It was not the most beautiful church, but then the Franciscans who built it embraced a humble simplicity that was reflected in the low, pitched roof, the plain brown brick and the large, somber, arching windows of green stained-glass. The school was connected to the church, and the sisters could walk to their convent along a short path beside a small, willow-shrouded hollow, next to a dirt road. In the hollow was a grotto to Mary. It was pretty—this little shrine—with its two wooden foot-bridges arched over a dry creek, flowers in bloom, a little waterfall spilling into a reflecting pool. In front was a rail to kneel before as you prayed and gazed up at the statue and waited for the miracle, for Mary to start weeping tears of blood.

Whether I was in school or not, the church and the school, the convent, the grottoes and fields and the small wood—this was a playground for me and my brothers and sisters and all of our friends. Our small, friendly neighborhood teemed with nearly a dozen families as big as ours and several more only a little smaller.

The church doors were always open, and we would sometimes sneak in when there were no services, tiptoe around (always whispering), wondering at the emptiness of it, the quiet. We would giggle and drink from the holy water decanter, or climb the stairs to the balcony at the back of the church—this being a particular risk, because we had always been forbidden to sit up there for mass, even if the church was packed full of people. We were *never* to go up there. My mother was very stern about this, and it makes me wonder if in earlier times there was a stigma attached to sitting up in the church balcony, that perhaps it was a place reserved for the sinners, the fallen. A kind of purgatory.

So there was the slightest thrill of mischief as you climbed those hard, cool steps and stepped out onto the creaking wood planks of the balcony overhang, easing stealthily past the five rows of pews and out toward the wrought-iron railing. When you had made it that far it was awesome the way the church spread out below you, your head nearly up in the wood-beamed rafters, the long aisle going up the middle, perfectly straight rows of pine pews stacking back toward and beneath you, a drowsy, summer afternoon light slanting in through the green, stained-glass windows, the smell of incense and candles seeping from the pores of brick and wood, all perfectly silent, the only sound coming from your own flaming heart—God's house.

Sometimes while we played in the grotto one of our favorite nuns would walk by and we would become teacher's pet, following these stern yet strangely kind women in their brown habits (their names antique, ornate: Sister Clarencia, Sister Theresita, Sister Felicity) into the dark hallways of the school. On rare occasions we were invited into the convent itself, for a piece of pie in the kitchen of the sweet, ancient nun who did all the cooking. Such a mysterious place. It was cool in summertime, big and with many rooms and quiet passageways, bright spaces and dark, reflective places, crucifixes and little shrines in every room: luminescence of candles casting soft light and shadows upon hard surfaces of brick and glass, linoleum, oak and pine—the common, comforting perfume of wax and furniture polish. It was so elemental that when things are difficult I dream of that place, the cleanliness and order, the long periods when there is nothing and after nothing to be followed by quiet and nothing more.

That was an innocent time. Of course there is no returning, but it is important to keep it within reach. I did not take it for granted, but even then I knew there was so much beyond that small, religious idyll that cradled me as a boy—there were deeper, darker things to discover, and it was only a matter of time before it became necessary to break away. Still, having grown up under the benign authority of that big, solemn bell, and having witnessed the almost monastic simplicity of the Franciscans—those nuns in their small, plainly furnished rooms: a bed, a nightstand, a window, a closet—it's enough for me now to know that it was there. It's a peaceful place I know I can always return to, if for no other reason than as a reminder that although the road is long and the landscape changes, you can go back to the *idea* of the past. Time can take away many things, but it cannot have the ideas in your mind if you hold onto them well enough.

And crowded as I am now in grief and detail, responsibility, the yapping jaws of doubt and subversive whispers of failure, I still dream of a room like that sometimes, a room as uncluttered and peaceful as the ones those sisters lived in, and a life apart. In my dream this room is a singular place, four walls, most importantly a window—even more importantly a door. All my possessions inside. One bill to pay—the rent—no banks or retirement funds, no credit cards or debts, no identification, no wallet even. A clean, bright space, no dust or dirt: scrubbed to a dull shine by an old woman who leaves the window open when she leaves. An easy job to support it, cash under the table and into my pocket, eating on the move—bread, cheese, a carrot, apples, milk and water, plenty of water—always moving, nothing hanging on or dragging behind, nothing loose: stealthy, silent, and lean.

When you stop moving, settle in one place, things start gathering on you. If you're lucky there are people that you love. Then your possessions become familiar and, finally, essential. Now there's an actual physical place, filled with people and things, where your life is. You get a job, feed money into it, and it grows. You construct an intricate web of insurance policies to protect it. This is my life now.

It's alright—I'm not complaining. Even though my wife is gone, there is still my daughter to bring along. Now it is her idyll I am tending. I'm a caretaker is all. It's fine. I can handle it—it's my pleasure really. Being Robin's father is exactly the kind of reward I've been searching for, a task requiring not a degree, no specific knowledge or skill nor a great deal of money—nothing but soul, humor, presence, the wisdom and strength to carve out a wide, safe place for her to roam free, a place she can return to as a reminder that although the road is indeed long, and the landscape changes, she will always have the idea of this time and place. We will grow some happiness here, preserve it in her heart, and she will always have it. She's going to need it.

But I need something too, some fresh air in my lungs, iron in my blood, or I won't be able to sustain all this for her. Despite this tragedy we've both endured and must live with, we can both be happy. There's room and time. It's not in my nature to fold up, acknowledge that love and happiness are gone, and plunge forward, joylessly. I wouldn't allow the hardness of life to overshadow the freedom of it, to let this big bump in the road I've come upon drive me to my knees as though I somehow deserved it all. I never understood Puritanism. How could a man continue to absorb the punishment of a hard life, strap the yoke on his back, his eyes downcast to the furrowed ground, and all the while praise a God who is supposedly vengeful and angry with him? That's like a dog wagging his tail for a man who beats him. Nope. Such a God would need to be defied with happiness.

God for me is kinder. I need to sit back, look all around me, and see that it's good. Some days are better than others. My little world is fine—my small, solid house, my back yard and the tall sycamore, my vegetable garden and flowers, my daughter and even the dog. But this is all Louise's world too, every inch. We built it all together. I was counting on her. We were both going to do this. When it's going badly I get bitter, find it hard not to resent the fact that I have to do it all by myself. When it's going well I feel guilt—like I borrowed half this stuff and now I get to keep it, maybe share it with somebody else. It seems wrong. It is wrong. I have riches I find difficult to enjoy because they were once ours, together. There are dozens of boxes in my basement with wedding gifts we never got around to opening.

She was the essential part. She came first, before everything else that I have. Her not being here—that's empty. Where does all that emptiness go? I don't think it goes anywhere. I think you're supposed to live with it. I think there are a lot of people who do. Maybe it's that emptiness we're here for. To stand apart and feel it, the thrill of it and the awfulness of it. To love and lose—that is a life lived completely. It's one of those things that is difficult to swallow but turns out alright in the end. Still, that is some painful experience. That was something painful—what Louise went through. To be slowly pulled away, watch it all fade before her, all that she loved: uncommonly slow and torturous. There was some hard learning going on there, something being communicated, something realized. Could a thing like that happen for no reason?

No, something was playing her. Some ancient premise was repeating itself, rolling ashore like a wave, powerful and incomprehensible. It seems silly to simplify it and you can't ignore it. So many things conspire to put us where we are. So much is determined. But there's a freedom to not being responsible, and you're free to defy it for as long as you can. Happiness is the best revenge.

18

I saw my first robin of spring today. Actually there were
two, looking well-fed and a little cold. It is still only March,
and nearly a foot of new snow fell over the last few days,
though now the air is warming again. Yesterday the snow
came whipping out of the east, a hard granular snow
blowing sideways, little shards of ice blown on a chilling
wind, stinging my ears and face and falling down the neck
of my coat. I was out again with Stella for her morning run:
every day in all weathers. She's impossible to live with if
she doesn't get her work. She loves the snow, was meant to
be a sled dog I think, has the size and look of one of those
half-crazed Huskies that pull the racers to Iditarod.

Most days I run her in a nearby park, watch her tear
around as I walk atop the small hill that rings a huge
athletic field. Today the wind came flying across the open
field and slammed into us as we walked along the far hill,
curling up clouds of snow that rolled up and over the lip of
the rise like apparitions, skulling the hilltop to the clean
frozen ground, depositing deep drifts on the downslope. As
I hopped foot to foot, stiffly, and turned my back to the

wind, trying to bury my head inside my coat, Stella dropped to an easy recline on the top of the hill and looked off straight into the teeth of it—her eyes black, thin, proud, oriental almost. She intently gnawed on the end of a large stick, oblivious to the howling cold—even relishing it—the gusts burying themselves in her thick, winter coat, twirling dimples into her fur, like crop circles.

True, she makes me crazy, but I love this dog. If you look at what she was built for, her yippy nerves are justified. Stella has some unsatisfied wildness in her—she wants to work. She needs a task and some responsibility. She needs a two-hundred acre ranch to patrol, something large enough to feed her rather ample paranoia, something for her to protect. It sounds silly—she's just a *dog*, I know—but I wish I could give it to her. She's happy enough, but she has more spirit than she's been allowed to express. All things in their most complete and perfect state, I do insist. A dog is best in all of its dogness—like a sports car is best when it's doing a hundred, or rock and roll is best when played loud. I like her dog-tired at the end of the day. There's nothing like a dog, warm and heavy with sleep after a long foray into the world, stretched out in a favorite corner of your house on a winter afternoon.

Robin and I had been watching out for the first robin of spring, and I had hoped we would see it together. But it was just the dog and I, out walking this morning, who came upon this pair of stocky, red-breasted songbirds perching in a small tree. They seemed to regard me with the same kind of pleasant surprise that I felt at seeing them, as though they were astonished that there were creatures who had stayed and survived the winter in this desolate place. Though the wind was biting, it was calmer this morning, sunny, the sky an ever-softer shade of blue, the clouds lighter, almost pink at the edges. As I watched Stella swim through the drifts like a porpoise, I found some hope in the subtle changes, reflected back on that span of sky only a month ago, when the blue was deeper and more ethereal, breathless, far—clouds not floating but shattered across the sky in the metallic cold.

Like this spring coming on, I am cautious and hopeful. It's going to be a while more. This last part can be the hardest, when you're so sick of your shelter, your cave, the mud and the frozen dust, the brown, hardened, ravaged earth, the scars. It takes work to undo all of this. It takes rain into soil. It takes time—those steady, cold, April rains, washing everything down, unlocking things, softening: things not even growing yet, still waiting, just waking up again to feel the earth around them. It is hard to have patience. You want everything to happen all at once, but a wise man said that time was invented to prevent everything from happening all at once. You'd be foolish to change that even if you could. It's a ride. Quit complaining. It goes around and around and you can only step back and admire it, the cycle of living and dying, being and not being. It's so old and powerful, so perfect.

Louise and I had some problems, as most couples do, but they are details not worth talking about—even boring. Typical relationship problems. There is going to be some static. Intimacy has a shadow, but Louise and I—we seldom let it catch up with us. What you need is two people who aren't going to panic when the shadow does move over them, who can give each other some room to keep moving so things don't settle and fester. When you stop growing you're dead, a piece of furniture. Marriage is dangerous that way. You see it all the time. One or the other stops trying. That's an awful thing to do to someone you supposedly love—declare yourself broken down and finished, drop your ever-widening ass down in the middle of your journey and say, "I'm done. Deal with me here." You've got to move fast and keep up. You've got to push one another into new territory, where life is fresh.

For almost our entire married life there was a lot of strain, to say the least. Less than three months after our wedding Louise was pregnant. We were trying for a baby—sort of. We knew we wanted one, but it still came as a shock, especially how it happened so soon. The first time we even thought about it, it happened. We were happy and frightened all at once, and as the idea settled down on us, on Louise especially, there was a little reorientation that needed to be accomplished. New roles, new plans for the future—mostly positive, but different and new.

Then, when her illness was discovered, we were knocked out of our orbit completely, jettisoned into space, spinning wildly. We never recovered. It was hard out there in space, though we kept it together. No time for dreamers anymore—that was probably the hardest part. We had been accustomed to living as children almost: carefree, a little reckless, no particular plan. Suddenly there was a child, and this horrible illness to contend with. That's a rather jarring introduction to reality for two people who had been avoiding it for the better part of their lives.

We found ourselves overwhelmed. We split the tasks as well as we could. Louise did more than anyone could have expected, a huge share. She wanted to do it—it was heroic the way she cared for Robin. I worked and filled in where I was needed. It was a lot to handle for both of us—a new baby, running a household, work, doctor appointments and hospitalizations—a never-ending stream of mundane details overridden by fear and occasionally punctuated by bouts of desperate terror. I tried to maintain a sense of normalcy, for all of us. I tried to manage things, arranged for help when we needed it. Louise's emotions were swinging wildly—you can only imagine—so I tried to be the steady one, tried to be the rock she said she needed.

Part of my responsibility was to take a beating now and then. Couples fight. We were no exception. Throughout our relationship I had always driven Louise crazy because she was more quick to argue, more overt with her anger. She would lash out, say what she wanted to say, and wait for a response. That was her way: honest, impulsive, inappropriate sometimes. Often I would deliberately not take the bait, wouldn't give her the fight she wanted. That was my way: more passive, evasive, *dirtier* probably. I see now that her way was healthier: get it out on the table, let it burn hot for a moment, confront it, then let it go. While she boiled, I stewed. She sought confrontation and I hated it. It was probably the one area we needed to work on: we needed to learn to fight fairly.

Her illness only accentuated this problem. The incredible grace that Louise displayed on the surface was masking what must have been a deep, black cauldron of horror below. It had to go somewhere. Only her strength kept it down. Think of it: in the span of about one year she was married, became pregnant, learned she had cancer, endured two surgeries, gave birth to her first child, and then, in the depths of the kind of post-partum depression all this would bring on, was started on a six-month chemotherapy treatment that brought on menopause.

And yet her public face was smiling, cheerful almost. She often found herself comforting the people who had come to comfort her. It was an act of generosity on her part to spare us her deepest terrors. And yet still it had to go somewhere. There were some rough moments, private moments of outrage and venomous hatred directed at her elusive, calculating enemy, moments that only I was witness to and that often became directed at me for lack of anyone else for her to turn upon. Of course, I wasn't having a picnic myself. I was miserable, but I knew, rightly, that nobody wanted to hear about it from me. "Just swallow it boy," I told myself. "It isn't personal."

There were opportunities to fight back. Only how do you fight with your wife when she's going through this? You just don't. You let her beat on you, and you take it. She hit me hard on a few occasions—not a physical beating but a mental one. She needed someone to point her anger at—I think I know a little bit about that now. Somebody had to take a beating and that somebody had to be me. At times I wished it could have been physical, wished she could just haul off and swing at me, punch and kick me in the head, arms, and shoulders with her fists, her small hands, until she was breathless and exhausted, sobbing, unburdened. Just beat it into me so that I could carry it for a while.

A sound, kinetic, physical beating would have been easier to bear than the slow, simmering resentment that came to reside between us even as we were fighting the enemy together. Our bond was strong, but this disease is so corrosive, so stealthy and lethal. It was like battle, things happening faster than you can acknowledge them. You get disoriented. You don't know how you got into this spot, but you look around and suddenly you're deep into it. We had built this life together and now there was this invader present, ruining everything for both of us. In a moment of panic you look at each other and think: *you*—it's because

I'm with you that all this is happening. It all started with you. If we had never met we would not be here together, watching our lives fall apart.

I understood this when she let me have it. I knew that I wasn't the enemy. But I had to play that role for her, because the real thing, the true enemy, was a thing without a face, a name, or even a soul, went about its killing with an almost disinterested, impassive method. There was nothing for her to strike at, so she laid into me. I never fought back. I can't decide whether it was my way of showing I loved her, or whether I secretly felt I deserved it. And I didn't feel heroic about it. It didn't make me feel any better. When she took it out on me, the only thing that could have made me feel worse would have been to fight back.

I have to go back to work soon, back to the routine, and now with spring coming on there will be more activities— picnics and roadtrips, backyard barbecues, flowers to plant and a vegetable garden to sow and tend to. The daylight will linger well into evening and yet with all the work the days will somehow seem shorter. This long winter in my cave has been a good thing, has worked like a dream in the way the body sleeps as the mind searches and sifts, solving things. I'm going to miss the time alone. It is time for something else.

My Louise is gone, gone, gone. It still does not seem real—or even possible—much less normal. I see her face, in photographs around the house, and find myself staring into them until I can almost summon her out from the frame to touch her, as though by my will and desire I can whip up the dust and make her appear, bring her home.

These empty rooms she once inhabited—how they haunt me still. When I was a boy a schoolmate of mine was killed in a car accident. Our teacher made the announcement in class one morning, and I remember for days after just looking at his empty desk with great skepticism. He had to be somewhere. Why didn't he just get up that morning as usual, come to school, and sit at his desk? That was his place. He should be there. I understood that his body had died, but where did *he* go?

I don't think my understanding of death has advanced much since then. People say it is the most natural thing. Come on. It is so *unnatural*. I refuse to believe in it. There is some vast deception going on around here, some cosmic joke. Just where the hell *is* Louise? Why doesn't she come home? I don't get it. It isn't funny.

I still fantasize vividly that she will walk in the door. One day I'm just standing in my kitchen, leaning up against the counter and having a cup of coffee. I hear the back door open and Stella, having heard it first and thinking there is an intruder, comes charging and barking out of her morning nap, ears up, weight forward, chest out. She rushes down the steps to the door until she recognizes who it is. Immediately she kicks down into her submissive greeting, ears back, head lowered, her whole body wriggling like a worm as she wags her tail so furiously.

I hear the voice first, though it is difficult over the roar of blood in my brain, the panic and thrill of thoughts in my head as I make the recognition. Also the dog is raising a huge commotion—high-pitched yips and howls, jumping and twirling, her tail pounding the walls in the narrow hallway. This dog-mistress reunion goes on for a few minutes (she is in no hurry): it is loud and emotional, Stella being our first "child" really. Louise and I had found her as a pup at a farm outside the city, and in the years before Robin was born we conspired to spoil the dog, a fact I am still paying for.

Finally she emerges from the darkness, bounds up the three steps to our kitchen. She gives me that wide, mischievous, unexpected-visitor smile, says simply "Hi!" as she walks toward me, arms wide. She's wearing jeans, her favorite old clop-around boots, an old sweater and jean-jacket I recognize. I wonder how she found those things, since I'd given much of her clothes away and the rest has been packed up in boxes in the attic for months. She looks beautiful, clean, well-rested (she should be). She looks like none of it had ever happened, her body whole and strong, her hair long again and shining, and gone from her face is the pain, or even the memory of pain. Her smile is awesome and real.

We kiss. How I remember that—like the smell of waking earth in spring the way it comes back. We embrace and hold each other for a long time, neither of us speaking. There is nothing to say and anyway we are both having the same thoughts, our minds in that familiar sync, together remembering, sympathizing, mourning, sharing.

The intensity of her feeling—I'm completely surprised by it. It almost knocks me off my feet, the way it comes back to me. I know the power of the feeling. I've been feeling it all this time. But I had grown accustomed to sending it off and never seeing it again, like sending radio signals off into space. Now she is right there, accepting, reflecting, sending it back—just as powerful but different somehow, fresher, the *scent* of her on it. Love is like a circuit that way. Two people connect and the light comes on.

And all I can say as I hold her and cry, my face buried in her neck, her cheek, her shoulder—all I can think to say (it

sounds silly, I know) is *thank you*. For letting me know—
however far away you may be, however out of reach—that
you feel it too. Because if you feel it then you are out there
somewhere. And if you are out there I will find you. Just
that single purpose can carry me through the rest of my life,
or even further. Even when I'm dead and gone, if I am still
me and you are you and canyons of eternity divide us, I will
never stop looking for you. You are fuel to go on forever. I
will find you.

Usually the fantasy ends there. Sometimes we gossip and
giggle about things that have happened since. We talk
about ordinary things like any couple. She notices I've
remodeled the kitchen. She admires the new hardwood
floor, the steel shelving and countertops, the fresh paint. Of
course we talk for a long time about Robin—how proud we
are as parents, how she is so like the two of us yet so much
herself—so silly and smart and charming.

She wishes she could stay until I bring Robin home from
school—wishes for it so badly that stars are born from her
wishing, far out in the ancient galaxies. And yet we both
know that this would only confuse our little girl, to have
this woman (almost a stranger, really), her mother, her
daddy's wife, home again in their house, holding her and
caressing her and cooing in her ear, only to have her
disappear again, leaving her longing for a mother—*her*
mother—open and raw and unfathomable again.

No, it won't do to have her stay. She must go back. Where
to? She can't say. Something about it—no words to describe
the place. But there is mischief in her eyes. Her smile tells
me something. She is healed and whole and that is enough
for me, for now.

And then just as suddenly as she arrived she is bounding
down the steps again. She turns and blows me a kiss.

"Goodbye sweetie!" she says. "But not farewell." And then she smiles softly as a sadness flashes across her face: "I'll see you again. Someday."

The door closes and she is just gone. And because it is a fantasy, I go back to sipping my coffee, smile and shake my head. If it were real I would probably want to chase after her, and it would all be starting over again.

19

The phone rang once, twice, and my father answered. I could barely make out the sound of his voice downstairs from where I lay in the half darkness. After a few minutes I heard him place the receiver down, and then there was a pause as he pondered. A dirty job. Of course only he could do it. Then I heard the slow, familiar *clop-clop* of his hard-soled size twelves picking themselves up and setting themselves down as he moved across the kitchen floor. When he reached the base of the steps there was another pause, a moment holding itself as though waiting for the turn of the Earth to catch up with it, and then finally there it was—the sound of my father's footsteps on the stairs.

I lay under the big blanket, eyes closed, listening to the sound of the end of something. Just this last, tiny thing to do. Just this news. It's going to hit me now. One more shot, one more big shot, and then it will stop. Nothing left after that. It can't hurt her anymore because she is no longer there. She did her part, and now I must do mine. Here it comes. Slow footsteps coming up the stairs.

The door opened. "Dave?"

"Yeah." My hands upon my face.

He came and sat beside me. News in his mouth like a dagger. How do you do it?

"That was your mother at the hospice," he said, and then he paused again as though he wanted to turn back. "Louise has died this afternoon."

I let out a big breath, the last breath of the first half of my life. "Okay," I said, and then I lay there quietly and wondered what to do.

He leaned down and reached his arms around me, put his head beside mine on the pillow. "Just cry," he said. So I did.

A couple of days after Louise died I had to call over to the funeral home about some detail concerning the wake. It was a Sunday. We were going to have visitation hours on Monday evening and then the memorial mass the day after. The man on the phone spoke in that concerned, hushed funeral home voice as we discussed our business, and in the middle of our conversation I had the strangest thought. *This man has my wife.*

Or at least what had once been my wife, the shell of her. She had been there for two days. They had driven in a hearse to the place where she had died, had gone into the room where she lay—two of them probably—and lifted her gently, her body stiff and inanimate now like a rack of bones. They had placed her in a black bag and pulled the zipper all the way around, wheeled her outside on a gurney, driven away.

And now they had her. She was there, probably in the basement of the building, probably not twenty feet from where this man was now standing as he spoke. She was still in her black bag, was laid out on a tray that receded into the wall, refrigerated like a piece of meat. It was not really her, of course, but it was close, the closest thing to Louise that we had left—the nearest approximation.

I thought *one last time*. I could go see her there, if I wanted to. Just once more.

I asked the man, "Is Louise still there?"

There was silence on the line—a surprised silence it seemed, as the man considered this. "Well...*no*," he said, the slightest crack, the tiniest sense of panic evident in his studied funeral home demeanor.

And I had a feeling I knew what this meant, but I had to ask, had to know. "Oh really?" I said. "Well...where has she gone?"

Another brief silence. The man was a bit unnerved. "We were told this was to be a *direct* cremation," he said finally. "The body has been taken to the crematory."

Notice this, I thought. I'm saying Louise. I'm saying her and she. He is saying body. He said the body.

"I see," I said. "Will she be cremated today then?"

"The body went over there this morning," he said. "So yes, I would think so. Yes."

I hung up and found myself wandering outside. It was another warm, sunny day, the sky deeply blue, the buzz of an airplane faint and distant. The crematory they had taken her to—I knew where it was. It was nearby. I pictured an oven door being opened, a fire white-hot and blazing inside, a box going in. My wife in that box.

I didn't cry or anything. I wasn't feeling too good, but then I had not been feeling too good anyway. Just a little more is all. I looked up into the sky and thought she could be flying over us right now. A big chimney and smoke coming out of that chimney and blowing over our house. I would never see her again. All evidence gone.

I thought, just burn then. Burn everything. Burn that miserable fucking disease, those maniacal cells. Burn every last one of them. She lives on but they do not. Burn them. Burn her pain and the bad times too, the tears. Burn her fear, the terror she felt for so long. All gone now, let them burn. All those jangled bones, that sheath of hers once beautiful, that temple become a prison—she is free of it now. She has flown. Burn it down.

And burn me too, or at least that part of me—the damage. Burn it away like surgery, that whole struggle, the futility of it, the effort and the wariness, the constant fear, for months and years the paranoia and the pain. It can do me no good anymore, can only weigh me down—cut it out and burn it clean.

Fire is a good thing, I thought. I have a long way to go yet but someday the whole world will end in fire.

Epilogue

Wounded. No real distinction in that. Just wounded and trying to care for it—like other people and their wounds—just cleaning it and bandaging it, trying to stave off infection, trying to keep it from spreading, looking for signs that it might be healing. Wounded in battle—I suppose it was bound to happen, even despite my relatively cushy post here, far to the rear in the ranks of the regiment.

It's more surprising I escaped harm for this long, I guess. Despite having endured this tragedy, I suffer no illusions that I am not still among the more fortunate souls on the planet, both in the having of something to lose and the capacity to endure the losing of it. Perhaps I should thank my Irish forbears for their hard-won, deeply ingrained capacity for enduring misery with a wry smile, a stoic nod, and an uncommon grace. Of course I would gratefully renounce this inheritance for my wife back and a general sense of panic, but I may as well try to pluck stars out of the sky. It's part of the story now. Without everything that came before, this moment would be far less worthy of our attention.

It really was a war. Now I've had my "emotional Vietnam" as Louise, in her inimitable way, would have put it. That war, well-documented in film and books and on the faces of angry, embittered men we occasionally pass on the street, has become synonymous in our time with the idea of ultimate horror, a hellish labyrinth that boys entered only to emerge—if they emerged at all—as hardened, wounded, haunted, even dangerous men.

And these are the survivors, the ones who have told us the story. What of those who did not make it home? What stories of awful loneliness, buried as they were amid the chaos and the suffocating fear—what harrowing tales were so unutterable that young men died to keep them secret?

In the months after Louise died a friend remarked at how well I seemed to be doing. I had been going through things in the house, took a couple of short trips, bought a new truck, started to remodel the kitchen. It may have looked like I was being "positive" (whatever that means), but in reality I was just plowing ahead, trying to put some of these events further behind, trying to move as fast as I could into the unfolding mystery still out there. There was a certain feeling of liberation. It was as though I had been dangling over a sea of shit for so long and now, having finally been dropped into the middle of it, I could at least start swimming for shore—some shore, anywhere.

And it seems as though when Louise died I really did split exactly in two. Almost immediately the one half picked up and started moving on—he was ready and prepared and knew there was nothing more he could do for her. Also he had big responsibilities literally pounding on the door. If he didn't let them in and at least try to start solving them, they would find another way in, probably in some rude and damaging manner.

But the other half of me stayed behind. That fellow is still there, lying in bed at his mother and father's house, the blankets over his face. I don't know if that is healthy. I don't really care. It was a big deal—what happened to him—and he is only trying to understand. Maybe he will continue to ponder it there, study it, try to learn something, and then finally he'll rise and catch up with the rest of me. Maybe he'll stay on.

I certainly don't know what's going to happen. It's kind of interesting, and there is no sense forcing the matter. The biggest problems seem to solve themselves when they're ready anyhow. I've always ended up better when I keep the hell out of it. I've got my mission now. I think I'll just point myself in the right direction, fold away this picture of my wife and daughter in my heart, and let the adventure continue. Time to loosen this rock and let go.

Just slide into the water with everyone else and disappear.